Ex Libris

St. Paul's Church

RICHMOND, VIRGINIA

Learning Through Liturgy

LEARNING
THROUGH
LITURGY

Gwen Kennedy Neville

AND

John H. Westerhoff, III

A Crossroad Book

THE SEABURY PRESS · NEW YORK

3290

1978 ·The Seabury Press
815 Second Avenue
New York, N.Y. 10017

Library of Congress Cataloging in Publication Data

Neville, Gwen Kennedy, 1938-
Learning through liturgy.
"A Crossroad book."
Includes bibliographical references.
1. Liturgics—Addresses, essays, lectures.
I. Westerhoff, John H., joint author. II. Title
BV176.N48   264'.001   78-17154   ISBN 0-8164-0406-2

Contents

Preface

This book addresses the questions surrounding the interplay between liturgical process and the processes of education—questions that have not been asked until recently in educational circles. In 1965 Massey Shepherd wrote *Liturgy and Education,* which dealt with some of these concerns; few others have addressed the subject before or since.

Our own interest in combining insights from our respective fields to attempt a broader understanding of educational questions began with our earlier work, *Generation to Generation.* In this book we joined the disciplines of cultural anthropology and religious education to introduce ideas on religious socialization, the learning of religions in and through social and cultural situations. One aspect of this earlier interest was in ritual and ceremonial occasions as opportunities for the teaching and learning of culture or of Christian faith. We now focus more specifically on the nature of liturgics and on the relation of liturgy to religious education.

The first half of this book, "Cultural and Community Roots of Liturgy," is a set of articles admittedly from the viewpoint of social-cultural anthropology. Each one is directed toward uncovering and clarifying the internal structure of ceremonies and celebrations in cultural and community life that have not previously been identified as liturgy or as liturgical forms. Gwen Neville has attempted to demonstrate here the ways these "folk liturgies" as she calls them operate as aspects of our religious tradition and experience.

The second half of the book, "Christian Life in Liturgical Context," is a collection of essays, admittedly confessional, in which John Westerhoff introduces four concerns related to catechesis and liturgics. None is fully resolved; however, each raises a pivotal question and points in the direction of an answer and its implications for ministry in the Christian church.

Our hope is that this collection will provide an introduction to liturgy and learning helpful to pastors, professional religious educators, students of divinity, and lay persons in the church.[1]

PART I

Cultural and Community Roots of Liturgy

Gwen Kennedy Neville

Introduction

The word *liturgy* has been defined traditionally in American English as prescribed ritual for public, formal religious services. The word could well be taken in a broader sense, however, to refer to the regularized and routinized aspects of daily life or of family and folk rituals and ceremonies. It is this more general, cultural meaning that I will adopt in Part I. My use of liturgy will encompass the informal patterns prescribed by culture for the regularized and repetitive forms of human behavior that fall into the general category of "ritual" or "ceremonial life." Webster's dictionary points out, in fact, that the roots of the word *liturgy* are the Greek *leōs* (people) and *ergon* (work). Liturgy could therefore be taken to mean "the people at work" or "the work of the people." In this sense, liturgy becomes action that is culturally patterned, and liturgics becomes the formalization of that action, while the liturgist is seen as the person who orchestrates the activities which themselves become embedded in the cultural grooves of a society or of a way of life.

In the first chapter of this section I have explored the outdoor services known to North Britain and to frontier America as a form of folk liturgy. These services, in spite of their antiestablishment and nonhierarchical underpinnings, have a patterned ritual form all their own which is rooted deep in the Celtic tradition of the sacred grove and the emphasis on nature as an aspect of religious experience. They are not merely historical curiosities, however. They are seen here as an example of informal liturgical structure and process that is as orderly to its participants and as correct in its theological propriety as the more strictly formal and literally prescribed services of the High Church tradition.

Chapter Two develops in detail the kin-religious gatherings of the Southern United States as ceremonial loci for the expression of culture and as the expression of a cultural theme I have labeled "religious familism." While this study was conducted only in the American South, its implications stretch out to enfold various regions and subcultures of our society. The Midwest is one area known for the same types of gatherings described here, an area where one finds the same cultural groups of Celtic and Anglo-Saxon ancestry found in the American South. New England, too, has a tradition of extended families reassembling from time to time, and religious communities exist for Methodists, Lutherans, Quakers, and others throughout the vacation areas of the country. This section, therefore, is intended to convey a sense of patterning and of regularity of cultural process that underlies many of the ritual gatherings that we have not previously recognized as liturgical in nature or religious in content. I have suggested in an earlier work that it is within the intense experience of these types of assemblies that children and adults learn and relearn their culture and/or their faith and practice. World view is developed and purposeful action formulated, not in the intellectual environment of the church school classroom but in the highly charged liturgical context of daily, weekly, and yearly events that combine the themes that are at the heart of the family and religious belief structure.

In addition to the cyclical events that pattern religious experience, the human being in a cultural-community setting also undergoes cycles of change and processes of transition in his or her own individual life cycle. These life crises have been studied and written about at length by both anthropologists and lay people as rites of passage, or life-crisis rituals. Baptism is given here as an example of one of these life-crisis rituals that has significance beyond the single life that is in transition. Rites of passage are also communal rituals as well as rituals for and about the movement of a person through a phase of growth. In Chapter Three baptism is seen as having ramifications for everyone involved.

Chapter Four addresses the problem faced by the student of culture, the anthropologist, who is attempting to study liturgical process with some objectivity while seeking to maintain her cultural ties and traditions. The difficulties involved in this marginal position may actually drive away potential observer-scholars from anthropology in particular because of the reliance of anthropology on methods of ethnography and participant observation. In this last chapter of Part I, I have drawn on my own experience to illustrate the potential problems and possibilities of this type of work by anthropologists interested in the analysis of ritual and of liturgical processes in our own society.

· 1 ·

Outdoor Worship
as a Liturgical Form

The outdoor meetings of the American frontier and the great field preachings of seventeenth-century Scotland and England have long intrigued students of religion and social history. American historians have dwelt on the camp meeting and "revivalism" as an expression of frontier spirit and as part of an individualistic temperament in the American mind of the period. Scottish historians have concentrated on the religious, historical, and political aspects of covenanting and of the covenanting tradition. Little attention, however, has been given to either of these types of events as cultural phenomena. This type of analysis, from the viewpoint of cultural anthropology, places the outdoor tradition in a new light—the structure and process of the separate types of services emerges as a liturgical form rooted in Celtic/Saxon tradition and having a prescribed order of its own. The liturgical form of the outdoor service has a number of variations and appears in several different historical contexts over a period of many hundreds of years. This chapter describes the elements that comprise outdoor worship as a tradition and the themes that appear and reappear in the content of the services. This form of liturgy is then contrasted to that of the indoor tradition, or the Established Church.

By viewing the outdoor service in terms of its liturgical form, it is possible to free the concept of liturgy from its restriction to formal ecclesiastical, indoor worship. It is also possible to begin to view the patterns of worship for the American colonial and frontier periods, not as historical aberrations resulting from a combination of social and psychological factors peculiar to that period but as expressions of an old and continuing cultural tradition.

In analyzing these events from an anthropological perspective it is important to place each one in the context of its historical occurrence and to attempt to establish the elements in the liturgy that form a recurrent pattern with a persistent regularity of structure and process. The questions asked of each type of service include those of location, use of space, time of scheduling, rhythmicity of recurrence, personnel attending, leadership, ritual materials used, order of action of people and of parts of the service, and the cultural themes that are repetitive. In other words: "Where is this event held?" "When does it happen and how often?" "Who comes?" "Who are the leaders and the participants and how is this leadership expressed?" "What kinds of worship aids are used (altar, table, cross, robe, hymnal, etc.)?" "What is the order of worship?" and "What beliefs, values, and meanings are most important?"

The events are well documented as history. No attempt is made here to do a scholarly history of these events or even to explain the historical transfer or continuous development into the American South. Instead, this chapter examines the structural and processual features of these types of events in contrast to the liturgical forms of worship and assembly congruent with established religion. This analysis is purposely limited to those outdoor assemblies which were stated specifically to be religious in nature, which exhibit continuity over time and regularity of occurrence, and which serve as the focal point for the gathering together of a specific bounded group of individuals. In Scotland, the historical covenanting meetings, field preachings, and open-air communions all fall within this definition, as do the outdoor services of the present day. In the southern United States the definition covers the tent meeting, the camp meeting, church homecoming, and graveyard reunion.[1] First the historical gatherings in Scotland are outlined and described, then the more familiar ones in the United States.

Scottish Outdoor Meetings in Three Centuries

The history of the introduction of Roman Christianity into Saxon and Celtic Britain is the story of a constant struggle of the Church Fathers to "civilize" the pagans, to obliterate their folk religion, and to bring into the sacred cover of the church edifice the numerous outdoor festivals and ceremonies accompanying indigenous belief systems. During the early centuries of the effort, seasonal festivals were gradually converted into Saints' Days, indigenous ritual forms were gradually secularized and turned into folk pastimes, and others were subsumed into medieval drama. The players and minstrels became professionalized as actors, removing them from the religious category. At the same time, however, the people's adherence to religious outdoor services of worship and to assemblies at sacred places such as stones, wells, trees, and glens continued to be important well into the medieval period and beyond. These practices were continually fought by the church through the centuries.

One strategy the church had for dealing with the problem of the indigenous religious practices was to tolerate these side by side with the practices of Roman Catholicism and to hope for the gradual disappearance of the earlier forms in the face of the missionary efforts. In a famous letter to Augustine, a missionary in southern England in A.D. 601, Pope Gregory stated the church policy as that of "weaning the people gradually from their heathen practices . . ." "The places of the pagan gods," says Gregory, "are to be purified, not destroyed, and the sacred places of the people are to be used for new worship." In his *Historia Ecclesia* the venerable Bede quotes Gregory's letter as stating: "The people may celebrate in arbors made of boughs of trees and built around the church whose especial festival is being celebrated."[2]

In later centuries, the church strategy changed to one that was not so tolerant. In the twelfth and thirteenth centuries, for instance, numerous decrees were sent out to ban the outdoor assemblies in an attempt to wipe out "pagan survivals." It is hardly surprising to find that in the wake of the Scottish Reformation when, again, the Established Church—albeit this time the Church of Scotland—set out to quell antiestablishment forms of worship and assembly, the target was the outdoor assemblage. This time it was in the form of the outdoor preaching or outdoor communions that abounded during the early seventeenth century in the Scottish Lowlands.

In the historical accounts of Scottish church conflict, one is struck by the recurring theme of outdoor versus indoor sites for worship, preaching, and communion services. Official church histories emphasize the field preachings and other outdoor services in the early 1600s, but long before this time the Celtic church in Scotland's Southwest possessed a tradition of outdoor worship and rural retreats. This region was, in fact, the cradle of Reformation participation. Many of the original Reformers in the Protestant Church of Scotland were from the South and Southwest of Scotland, where the Scottish church had a history of over a thousand years.

The Celtic church, begun by St. Ninian in the fourth century in the Southwest, emphasized nature and the beauties of the outdoors. Withdrawal to the woods or lakes for meditation by groups of Christians was a regular part of the liturgical tradition, according to Chadwick, noted historian of Celtic Britain.[3] Chadwick states that the Celtic saints were sanctified, not by ecclesiastical authority but by their own daily lives and the respect of their fellow Christians. If sacred stones, wells, and trees of pre-Christian religious forms were a problem to this branch of early Christian tradition, they were assimilated. Stones, wells, and trees were incorporated into a Christian form of worship that emphasized the beauty of nature and the virtues of the simpler outdoor rural life. Throughout the next centuries these elements of rural simplicity and natural beauty focused on certain sacred places became central to the Scottish outdoor worship service as a liturgical form.

Three basic types of meetings will be described here: the covenanting meetings of the 1600s, the communion season of the 1700s and 1800s, and the conventicle or outdoor service of the present day. Each is dealt with as a liturgical event within a historical context and in a sequence of cultural continuity.

Covenanting in the 1600s
The outdoor form of worship emerged as a form of protest during the period following the formation of the Protestant church in Scotland in 1560. In the second half of the sixteenth century and throughout the seventeenth century, war ensued between the Reformers, later the Covenanters, and the Established Church. During this

period, from time to time, various preachers who had been branded radical were ousted from the pulpit of established churches by order of the king, and their followers rallied round them in the open fields to hear even more radical sermons and in some cases to marshal forces for battle against the king's armies.

Local histories disagree on where and when the earliest of the covenant meetings, later known as conventicles, took place. All agree that the movement began or came to the surface in the Southwest. The name Covenanters came from those who had in 1638 signed the National Covenant in Greyfriars Church, Edinburgh, to abolish the episcopacy; but it was later applied to all followers of the movement. The covenant preachers were ousted from the churches officially in 1661 and official curates inducted to take their places.[4] At the same time field preaching became a capital offense. All ministers were required by law to live more than twenty miles away from the parishes they had formerly served. There were many bloody battles, and thousands died; at the same time many of the offenders were also exported to North Carolina or other colonies for their crimes.

In writing a local history of the Galloway region, Robertson describes the situation as follows:

> In 1662 Gabriel Semple, minister of Kirkpatrick-Durham was driven from his church . . . he conducted services in Corsock House until his audiences became too large, then in the garden, and finally in the open fields. . . .[5]

Robertson gives the figure for excommunicated ministers as 350 throughout Scotland during this period. The so-called Black Act of 1670 made even the attendance at conventicles punishable by death and also leveled heavy fines on those who did not attend the parish church where they were registered.

In spite of these legal sanctions, attendance swelled, with the most famous service of the period coming in 1678 at Irongray Churchyard, drawing several thousand to take communion in the open air. Robertson describes the setting at this famous service in this way:

> The tables were four parallel rows of long flat oblong stones, each row about 20 yards in length. At one end there was a circular cairn of stones several feet high where the officiating minister stood. The communion was served in relays to several hundred communicants at a time, and the service continued all through the day and into the evening.[6]

The services at Irongray lasted three days, "a great open-air communion service . . . the rude stones forming the communion tables and the seats."[7] Eventually it was this aspect of the covenanting tradition—the outdoor communion—that became firmly incorporated into the ecclesiastical calendar of the rural churches in the Scottish Southwest and borders.

Communion Season—1700–1850
In the century following the great covenanting meetings —the century of early manufacturing and of emigration to the colonies—the open-air tradition continued in the form of the outdoor communion in the country parish. "Communion season" is referred to throughout the literature of the eighteenth century as that week in the summer, in May, or in October, when the individual country parish held its gathering for the outdoor service. Each parish had a set time for the holding of its communion, and the times were orchestrated in such a way that

members of adjoining parishes might attend if they so desired.

Since the days of the Reformation, one method of bounding off the group who received the communion together was the issuance of tokens, or small circles of carved wood carrying the seal of a particular parish. These would be issued by the minister to communicants in the one parish, and when they moved, they would present the token to the minister in the new parish as evidence of good character and church membership. A verbal and spatial statement known as "fencing the tables" began with the reading of Scripture, denying the sacraments to those who were not true believers. At the same time, the tables were actually fenced off so that direct access of the people was denied. Elders were stationed at the entry to the tables to receive people's communion tokens as proof of their status in the community of the redeemed.

From a museum exhibit in Kirkudbright the following information gives a picture of the seriousness of the exclusion process.

> In a parish in Perthshire in 1791, 2361 people took communion at one service. . . . It was customary in those days for the communion table to be enclosed within a wooden paling to keep out non-communicants. . . . An elder stood at one end to collect tokens.[9]

A local historian, J. J. Vernon, examined the kirk records for the Parish Kirk of Hawick for the period 1711–1725 and found numerous references to the communion season. He found that prior to 1700 the Kirk Session was strict in seeing that tokens were given only to members of their own parish. Subsequently, however, it became a common custom for people of adjacent parishes to come in large numbers to any church in the district where the communion was to be observed. In order to provide the visitors with tokens, the minister of the parish would supply the ministers of adjoining parishes with tokens several weeks before. It was the custom of the country folk to attend several communions, and farm servants contracted with their employers to be allowed to attend a specified number of fairs and communions per year. It was a social occasion where one visited with friends and kinfolk as well as listened to the preaching and partaking of the bread and wine of the sacrament itself.

The service was held in the kirkyard. Vernon found references in church records to payments made to tradesmen for putting up tents and tables. He notes the picturesque scene created by the "tables laid out on trestles on the grass." At Hawick the communion season was the first Sunday after the ingathering of the harvest, in October. The event lasted three days, Saturday was the first day, the communion being held on the Sabbath, a service of Thanksgiving following on Monday. Because the communion season in Hawick was in October, the weather was too cool for sleeping in the open fields, so travelers either came early in the morning and went home late at night or they stayed over in local inns. The visiting ministers slept at the manse.

Another local historian, James Russell, describes the communion season at Yarrow in the early 1800s as follows:

> Our own Communion was one of our happiest seasons. There were holidays and no lessons. There were friends about the house, and good dinners. . . . My father had just *one* Communion in the year, in the beginning of August (latterly on the second Sabbath of July). In this he conformed to the custom

of those days; and, I believe, was influenced by the feeling prevalent in many quarters still, that it had the sanction of the Mosaic dispensation in its yearly Passover, and the belief that it was observed with more solemnity than it would have been had it been celebrated more frequently.[10]

Russell states that the services before and after the communion were a major focus of emphasis and, in fact, the gathering was commonly known among the country people as "the preaching." The sequence of events is described by Russell for the communion of his own childhood, held by his father as minister.

The Sabbath service was a protracted one. It began at 10:30 and with one hour and a quarter of interval, did not close till about 7:00 P.M.; so that those who came from the extremities of the parish, . . . had to start at an early and return at a late hour. There were seven full communion tables. Refreshments of bread and cheese and milk were provided in the kitchen for all comers of the people generally; a bowl put in the "ministers' well" for those who liked a cooling beverage of spring water; bread and ale in the barn, furnished by some of the publicans of the parish; . . . and refreshments in the dining room and parlour of the manse for the farmers and their families. The ministers and elders dined at the manse during the interval. A sumptuous "Monday's dinner" to which some of the principal parishioners were invited, completed the service of carnal things.[11]

During the gathering, there were many who, according to contemporary reports, became quite rowdy with the mixture of fellowship and strong drink. Russell refers to the situation in a certain parish—not his native Yarrow—where in 1785 he considers the assembly to have "degenerated" into a social occasion.

... the crowds needed refreshments, "lest they should faint by the way" . . . baps of bread and ale were planted round the churchyard dyke [wall]. All day long there was an oscillation between the one and the other.

When a popular preacher mounted the rostrum, the people all flocked to the tent; when a *wauf* hand turned up, the tide was all the other way. . . . The tent was deserted, and the baps and barrels carried the day. There was an unceasing contest between the spiritual and the spirituous.[12]

It was the social occasion and merriment of the outdoor gatherings that led the poet Robert Burns to compare the event to a country fair. There are in fact many similarities if one examines carefully the social meaning and the sequence of events. It cannot be ignored that the two appear side by side in the farm labor contracts of the period in terms of guaranteed time off for leisure pastimes. On the other hand, the communion cannot be passed over lightly as merely a social gathering for visiting with neighbors. Over the centuries it took on a symbolic meaning, ceremonially connecting the living community with its past in the covenant tradition, the Celtic church, and the feasts of the Old Testament. The beauties of the countryside were extolled as being a part of God's creation, and the sacredness of of the place itself was emphasized by references to previous holy men holding the pulpit of the church and to the godly lives of the ancestors who were buried in the graveyard.

The symbolic significance of the open-air communions is touched upon in this poem written in the nineteenth century by a Hawick parishioner. It underlines the importance of the past and of the continuing community of people within one parish throughout the ongoing generations.

Slow the people round the table
Outspread, white as mountain sleet,
Gather, the blue heavens above them,
And their dead beneath their feet;
There in perfect reconcilement
Death and life immortal meet.

Noiseless round that fair white table
'Mid their fathers tombstones spread
Hoary-headed elders moving,
Bear the hallowed wine and bread,
While devoutly still the people
Low in prayer bow the head.[13]

As late as 1845 we know that open-air communion services were routinely celebrated annually—at least in the Southwest. In the Second Statistical Account of Scotland, published in 1845, the Reverend Cullen and the Reverend Murray describe the Balmaclellan church building as "much too small for sacramental occasions, when worship is performed in the open air. . . ."[14]

After the turn of the century in both the Southwest and in the Borders, however, there appears to be a shift of the communion to the inside of the church building. Residents in the region today are unable to recall seeing an outdoor communion service in their lifetimes. This may be due in part to the gradual increase of influence of the Church of Scotland General Assembly in reuniting smaller segmented factions into an overall national church structure. The official policy is now to hold communion four times a year and to hold it within the prescribed indoor liturgical form of the Book of Church Order.

Jubilees, Anniversaries and Conventicles: 1850–1975
Outdoor services from 1850 through the present day take
on the form of anniversaries, jubilees, or conventicles.
These are gatherings celebrating the anniversary of the
founding of a local church, the anniversary of the coming of the present minister, or an anniversary or a covenanting battle. The two former types are often celebrated on twenty-fifth and fiftieth anniversaries, thus
adopting the name "jubilee." The outdoor commemora-
tions of covenanting battles are held annually on the date
of the battle and are known by the people as conventicles
or simply as "outdoor services." Again, a recurring
theme is the tie to the past and to the continuous community of God's people who have inhabited this particular
place over the unfolding years.

Frequently a local history is written by the pastor to
commemorate these anniversaries—especially those on
centenaries. One such local history written in 1889 describes a jubilee held to commemorate the anniversary of
a minister's ordination—apparently the seventy-fifth, although it is unclear whether the honoree was alive or
dead at his celebration.

> An outdoor meeting under a tent held to commemo-
> rate the third jubilee of the ordination of Reverend
> John Hunter . . . at Gateshaw Brae . . . a crowd of 2000
> from all the Border Presbyteries, from the Free
> Church, from the Presbyterian Church of England.
> Some were present who had attended a similar
> gathering fifty years ago.[15]

Apparently Gateshaw Brae was chosen because of its
long history of having been the scene of outdoor services.
It is especially mentioned in connection with the outdoor meetings held during the secession of 1737. In this

dispute, those who wanted to keep the right to choose a minister in the hands of the local congregation and among heads of families rebelled against the General Assembly. The official body had ruled that this right to choose a minister was to be restricted "to heritors, elders, magistrates and town councillors in burghs and to heritors and elders in country parishes."[16] As in other disputes throughout the splitting and realigning of factions that marks the history of the Church of Scotland, the rebellious groups in this disagreement took to the open air.

Today a number of outdoor services in summertime commemorate activities of Covenanters and their organizational (or antiorganizational) counterparts. In the Lammermuir hills there are several meeting spots made famous by protestors who withdrew from the parish church at Lauder in 1747 to form an outdoor group affiliated with the "Anti-Burghers", as the secessionist movement was called. They are referred to locally as "the lineal representatives of the Covenanters." Another famous outdoor service is held annually at St. Mary's Loch at an old graveyard. The gathering is known as a "blanket preaching" (a Covenanter is quoted as having preferred outdoor worship "on the blanket of the Lord.") The rhetoric of the preaching at summer gatherings of these types often includes references to the previous generations who "fought oppression." Among the ministers inside the established town churches, however, and in the theological schools at Edinburgh and Glasgow, the meetings are largely scoffed at or ignored. If noticed at all, it is with the cryptic comment of one established churchman who referred to the blanket preaching as "an old tradition being dragged along."

Outdoor and Indoor—Some Recurring Themes
In this sketchy reconstruction of over three hundred years of outdoor services, it is possible to discern several repetitive themes and a number of structural regularities. Consistently, outdoor services are associated with the rebellion against authority and hierarchy represented by the Established Church. They represent a political statement as well as a theological statement. The emphasis is on nature and sacred places, many of which are also connected with the sanctification of hallowed ground by battles "for freedom" or "against oppression." Heroes and ancestors is honored in the preaching, in the celebration of anniversaries, and in the holding of gatherings at the gravestones of well-known covenanting figures. The collective community of the ancestors is honored in the act of holding services in the graveyard "with the dead around their feet." The participating group is distinct and bounded—in the past by fenced tables, in the present by selective knowledge and an interest in finding out the repetitive exact day of the gathering and attending it.

Contrasting to the antiestablishment expressions of the outdoor services are the staid, stalwart, formal services held inside the Established Church of Scotland. The pattern of liturgy remains essentially unchanged over the centuries, and the doctrine preached is the approved version of intellectually refined Calvinism that is taught in the seminaries at Glasgow and Edinburgh. There are no bishops and no patronage in the modern-day Church of Scotland. Each congregation chooses its own minister and sends representatives to the regional Presbytery and to the General Assembly. Whereas the minister is "called" by the congregation, he is not a member of it but is a member of Presbytery and subject to his ultimate regulation by Presbytery and by the General

Assembly. The system of government, theological orthodoxy, and organizational structure of the Church of Scotland is both indoors and closed.

Outdoor Services in the Southern United States

Beginning with the journals of earliest settlers to the southern colonies, there are references made in various ways to outdoor assemblages for worship. These were held in the open air at first due to the lack of any meetinghouses. It is important to note, however, that the outdoor tradition of the Covenanters was brought to the Carolinas very early with the hordes of Lowland Scots who were exiled from Scotland for their antiestablishment activities. They came in through the ports at New Bern and Wilmington, N.C., and Charleston, S.C. They came down the wagon road through the Shenandoah Valley on to the Carolina Piedmont. The peak years of settlement by Scots and Ulster Scots were the years 1710–1790.[17]

In the centuries between early settlement and the Civil War, approximately 150 years, the southern United States was the scene of the same kinds of outdoor-indoor dichotomies that characterized the British church. The communion and its associated preachings went outdoors in the American South in several different types of events. Those treated here include (1) the tent meeting, (2) the campmeeting, and (3) church homecoming.

Methodists and Outdoor Preaching
One outdoor type of service corresponds roughly to the rebellious field preachings of the Covenanters. This was the outdoor preaching held by early Methodists. Like

their Scottish brothers of the previous century, the earliest Methodist rebels were ordained ministers in the Established Church—in this case the Church of England. They were expelled, however, one by one as they preached their radically antiestablishment ideas and demanded reforms that were unpalatable to the church hierarchies. Throughout Georgia and North Carolina, where the Church of England dominated both the religious and secular life of the 1700s, the radical preachers were relegated to the church steps, the town square, and later, after being expelled from the towns altogether, to the open fields.

On the frontier in Tennessee, Kentucky, and North Georgia the outdoor tradition continued and flourished. Two types of outdoor evangelistic services held by famous preachers were (1) the tent revival, or "tent meeting," and (2) the camp meeting. Both of these traditions continue today.

The tent meeting or tent revival was aimed at evangelizing the unsaved, bringing religion to the unchurched, and in general herding the wild sheep of the frontier into flocks with a shepherd at their head. If this was properly accomplished by a traveling preacher, a group of the saved could then be gathered into a continuing congregation, thus bringing the outdoor meeting indoors. The saved individuals would eventually enclose their service themselves by building an edifice over the top of the meeting place and becoming institutionalized as a Methodist church.

The second tradition, that of the campmeeting, is related to the tent revival only by virtue of its evangelistic basis. The camp meeting became a part of the frontier religious pattern as a recurring assembly, once a year in August for all the scattered members of a set group of families who also attended Methodist churches indoors every Sunday. Campmeeting grounds dot the country-side of North Georgia and East Tennessee, where for the past 150 years prescribed groups of members have regathered for a week annually to hear preaching services and to visit with their kin and friends. The central feature is usually an open-sided structure known as the arbor, in honor no doubt of the brush arbor constructed to cover the heads of early frontier Methodists who were sent outdoors by the Established Church.[18]

Church Homecomings and Other Gatherings

While the circuit-riding preachers on the frontier continued to hold their outdoor preachings, church buildings became the center of congregational community in the settled neighborhoods of Virginia, North Carolina, and Georgia. The church at the center of the scattered community is a typical pattern for all the denominations in the South with the exception of the Episcopal, which remained tied to towns, plantations, and heavily settled urban areas.

Throughout the 250 years of their history, these scattered country churches have held various versions of an annual outdoor reunion of the members, drawing those born and reared in the congregation who have moved away. The reunions are referred to in all denominations as church homecomings, anniversaries, or reunions.

In the Presbyterian congregations of the 1700s the communion could be served only periodically in those congregations lacking a full-time pastor, so the communion would be given once or twice a year when an ordained minister was sent out by the Synod of Philadelphia. The occasion would be shared by several neighboring congregations and, as in Scotland, would last for three or four days.

In most of these outdoor gatherings today—the church homecomings and reunions—the emphasis is not on the sacrament but on the "communion of the saints" or the "fellowship of the people." Today at such gatherings the tables are still set out on the church lawn adjacent to the graveyard, but the elements of the symbolic meal are no longer the bread and wine. For this fellowship occasion, known as "dinner on the grounds," the assembly shares a special ceremonial feast consisting of fried chicken, vegetables, pies and cakes, and iced tea, all of which is prepared and brought to the dinner by the mother of each participating family. If the Sacrament of the Lords Supper is a part of the gathering, it is celebrated inside the church during the regular service of worship and preaching. Outdoors, after the service, the people pass down the stone or concrete tables laden with food, fill their plates, and partake of this communal meal together.

Within the activities of a homecoming gathering, the themes of the sacred place, the founding fathers of the congregation, and the ancestors buried in the graveyard are all present. The past and the present are tied together in ways similar to the past and present being restated in the Scottish outdoor meetings.

Variations on the church homecoming assembly have been reported for West Virginia, where the gathering is known as a "graveyard reunion" but exhibits the same features; for Alabama, where a similar occasion is known as Decoration Day; and for East Tennessee where a gathering is known as a Graveyard Association Day. All of these center on the ancestors and on being aware of the work of holy forebears. In the church homecoming gathering there is an implicit emphasis on those saints who have gone before, and people often include visits to the graveyard as part of their return to the old home church. Homecomings, like outdoor communions in Scotland, are often held in the graveyard itself. In rural churches these events are universally outdoor rather than indoor gatherings. Both homecomings and camp meetings are further discussed in the next chapter.

Summary

A careful examination of the internal structure and process of the outdoor services of Scotland and the Southern United States reveals a consistency of pattern and form that constitutes a specific liturgical tradition in itself, similar to that of Celtic Christianity and its indigenous Celtic religious antecedents. The outdoor worship service has persisted as an important type through many centuries of Scottish history and has been carried by Scots and North Englishmen into the Southern United States in several manifestations.

Covenanting services, communion on the church grounds, twentieth-century conventicles, Methodist frontier revivals, camp meetings, and church homecomings all can be seen as aspects of this ongoing tradition. These services and field preachings are not isolated occurrences with only historical particularistic significance. Instead, they constitute a form of cultural expression that corresponds to certain folk cultures of northern Britain. As such they exemplify a ritual form which finds its distinctiveness in opposition to the hierarchical forms of the Established Church and to the "Great Tradition" of Roman and continental Christianity. The social organization of the folk—that of scattered communities centered in crossroads meetings—finds itself in counterpoint with the social organization of highly stratified feudal society and of the exclusive and monopolistic structures of the *burgh* or town. It is the particular liturgical form of the outdoor service that the populous seized upon through time to express its own cultural identity over against the hierarchies of both the feudal domains and the feudal-economic captivity of the towns whose form of worship was that of the well-established and traditional hierarchical state church.

The symbolic center of the indoor tradition is the altar, or the communion table. The symbolic center of the outdoor tradition is the table around which all the saints gather together for partaking of a meal made of common food. The rural Protestant churches of the American South—whether Baptist, Methodist, Presbyterian, or one of the fundamentalist groups—share an important architectural feature. It is the outdoor tables, now made of concrete blocks or of concrete and stone, where the congregation and its constituent kin groups gather together for "dinner on the grounds"—or the "communion of the saints."

The categories used here for analysis of the types of events have included the following: location, or space-use; time, rhythmicity of recurrence; personnel in attendance; organization of leadership; ritual materials used; order of action; and cultural themes. Using these devices as tools for organizing, the categories have been summarized here for the two contrastive types of service, the outdoor and the indoor.

	Outdoor	*Indoor*
1)	open-air (field, tent, or churchyard)	inside church building (permanent structure)
2)	congregational emphasis	hierarchial levels emphasized
3)	shared communal meal (may be ordinary food as in church homecomings)	sacramental food (bread and wine) blessed and served only by ordained priests

Outdoor	Indoor
4) emphasis on "fellowship" and on "communion of saints"	emphasis on centrality of sacraments or of doctrine
5) emphasis on ancestors	emphasis on biblical and ecclesiastical history
6) emphasis on local sacred place (the church, the graveyard, the location of an historic event)	emphasis on the institutional Church, the Church ecumenical, or the denomination as the locus of identity.

In terms of their cyclical recurrence, the outdoor services usually occur annually and in summertime. Their "fit" into an informal liturgical year based on agricultural cycles expresses a cultural interpretation of time. In the folk liturgies as well as in more formal ones, time is culturally segmented into symbolic units. The arrangement of these services around the summer season, or the spring-to-fall seasons, presents an intriguing contrast to the more regularized repetitive pattern of the ecclesiastical liturgical calendar and to the precise week-to-week regularity of the indoor worship service.

In this chapter I have presented outdoor services as a specific liturgical form in contrast to that of indoor worship. This specific form of liturgy expresses continuing cultural themes centered around equalitarianism, naturalism, localism, and an additional theme that I will call "religious familism." This theme emphasizes the local kin group and its ancestors and deemphasizes the formal doctrinal, biblical, and ecclesiastical historical concerns. In Chapter Two this phenomenon is examined in detail for the American South.

Folk Liturgies
in the American South [1]

Two kinds of liturgy can be found in every culture—
the formal ritual and the informal or folk liturgies.
Formal worship in the strict sense and highly regularized ritual in preindustrial societies are considered to
belong to the formal liturgical tradition associated with
the practice of religion. Folk liturgy, on the other hand,
could be identified as the set sequences of daily, weekly,
or other recurrent regularized forms of prescribed behavior for certain events, not necessarily religious.

One example of folk liturgy is the regularized set of
prescriptive behaviors for a dinner party in our own
society. This prescription includes timing, manner of
serving, appropriate conversation topics, categories
of food normally served, type of seating (at a table or on
the floor), arrangement of people at the meal, the dress
of these people, the way they hold their forks and knives
and which fork they use in what order, and many other
specific details that are understood by all the participants
within any one cultural setting. An anthropologist from
Mars observing and describing an American dinner
party could predict with some degree of success the repetitive pattern that would be expected at every other
dinner party within that social-cultural group. The
nightly ritual of families having their normal weekday
dinner—known in the South as "supper"—is more
relaxed than the prescribed form for the formal dinner,

yet many of the same rules apply and the observing anthropologist would quickly discern that these are two subtypes of one type of event. In this chapter some of the folk liturgies of the American South are explored as event types that carry specific sets of rules and regulations for their participants and that serve to express cultural themes central to religion and family life in Southern culture.

One of the distinctive features of the white Protestant culture of the American South is its emphasis on family ties, entwined with an emphasis on religion. These two themes appear and reappear in Southern literature and in historical and social science analyses of the region.[2] Among Presbyterians the phrase "kirk and clan" is often used to express the configuration of world view and activities which make up a way of life that is deeply ingrained in American Southern patterns and styles, reaching backward in time to Celtic and Anglo-Saxon ancestors. The kirk-and-clan image and ideology, however, is not limited to the Presbyterians or to descendants of the Scottish colonists. Instead, it pervades Methodist, Baptist, and other Protestant groups of British and North European origins; it expresses a loyalty to living kin, to ancestors, to a home place in a rural area or small town, and to the great family of faith embodied in a local congregation and in a larger denominational identification. The two themes of family and religion form such basic threads in the fabric of life among these Protestant people that they are used here as the central focus in this exploration of folk liturgy. The twin themes are expressed specifically in recurrent gatherings. These gatherings, including family dinners, reunions, church homecomings, and campmeetings, are both family-oriented and religious in nature. They state symbolically the central beliefs and values associated with the family and church in Southern Protestantism.

In order to assign a label to this matrix of beliefs, meanings, and behaviors, I have used the term *religious familism.* This term acts as shorthand to refer to an elaborate set of cultural patterns and processes. It has been chosen because it summarizes the idea that the Southern family system is more than its kin-oriented activities and beliefs, though kin-relatedness is a major aspect of southern manners and morals. The religion of Calvinistic Protestantism underlies the construction of the family as a part of a greater family of the saved, or a family of faith. The family is frequently referred to in religious terms, with the Christian family viewed as the nucleus of a greater church family belonging to the community of faith. In the same manner, the church is often referred to as a family, with God as the father and Jesus as the brother of humankind. In the eyes of God, the people of the church are children, spoken of as children of God. Family ceremonies are opened and ended with prayers, and individual life crises are celebrated within family-centered rituals held in local church congregations.

Religious familism is not only associated with the rural people of the frontier and of the farm, although it has full expression among both groups, but it is also a part of the culture of southern elites—the Piedmont industrialists, both owners and workers; the college professors and other professionals; and the emerging urban middle class. It exists among small town Protestants in every corner of the South as a region and among former rural and small-town people who have moved into commercial-industrial cities over the past several generations.

The Study of Kin-Religious Gatherings

In order to develop the understanding of a cultural theme being expressed in recurrent ritualized events, four different gatherings are presented here, each of which gives expression to the phenomenon of religious familism. These gatherings include the family dinner, the family reunion, the church homecoming, and the campmeeting. The first two gatherings focus on the family itself and on the repetitive reestablishment of family ties among scattered people. The second two have the church or the campmeeting (the outdoor church) as their central focus, reassembling scattered members of a congregation or of a campmeeting constituency. In both kin-centered and church-centered gatherings, however, the two themes of family and religion are inextricable.

Each of the gatherings is presented here in terms of its personnel (Who comes?), rhythmicity of occurrence (How often?), location (Where?), space-use (How are people arranged?), its internal structure of action (What happens in what order?), and its use of sacred symbols. This ethnographic study of gatherings extends the descriptive data on Southern culture, but also it extends the use of a particular model. This model is useful for understanding informal liturgical tradition and for understanding the relation of ritual life to religious education. Urban dwellers are seen here as scattered, recurrently reassembling, family-religious communities. The children of these urban families are exposed, through recurrent participation in reunions and other gatherings, to the way of life of their Protestant culture and are taught certain core meanings and beliefs.[3]

In an earlier work on religious summer communities, I studied the processes of ritualization and symbolization of family and church values within one group of Southern Protestants, the Presbyterians at Montreat, North Carolina. Continuing research has established that the same processes identified in the Presbyterian summer community are a central feature of family and church life throughout the Piedmont and the coastal South and that the participation in recurrent family-religious gatherings extends to all three of the major denominations of the region.

The original study at Montreat uncovered an annual cycle of withdrawal to a rural mountain retreat center by large numbers of Southern Presbyterians. The main activities there were family visiting, religious study and worship, and participation in a well-planned round of clubs and groups aimed at socialization of the young. This summer retreat center is only one of dozens of such summer havens of various denominations, many within a short distance of Montreat, where religious familism finds full expression. Within the overall community processes of summer retreats, however, are embedded other smaller scaled events geared to one family's gathering to honor their own ancestry and to express loyalty to their kin. This type of family-centered gathering has been found throughout the South among all denominations. In addition, gatherings associated with rural churches and campmeetings seem to embody many of the characteristics of the Montreat gathering.

My students and I have observed and recorded numerous events of this type, a class of events giving social form to the idea of religious familism. We have called these events "kin-religious gatherings," including both family and church gatherings which share certain crucial features. These features include the central focus on family and religious ties and loyalties; a meeting place that is rural, "natural", or in some sense apart from daily routines of the participants; the choice of a recurrent day in summer or of a recurrent religious holiday as the time; and the presence of a network of scattered individuals who are linked by kinship, friendship, and common religious heritage but who may be together as a group only on these occasions.[4]

While the four gatherings presented here share features that are highly regular and repetitive, there are numerous variations based on denominational difference; region, rural or town location; and the socioeconomic status of the participating group. Denominational differences are especially noticeable, and the town and country differences are marked, both between and within denominations. Before turning to the types of gatherings, it is useful to look more closely at these denominational differences as they take social shape in Southern culture.

The Presbyterians are most easily recognizable as forming a group that is historically and culturally separate from other Southern denominations. Southern Presbyterians cling to a Scottish historical heritage and a confessional dogma that has resulted in a selectivity of clergy and leadership. The central feature of the theology is the belief in the sovereignty of God and the salvation of grace resulting in an elect group of God's people. During colonial times and in the early days of the American Republic, Presybterian emphasis on an educated clergy gave the denomination a certain exclusiveness, while many fringe congregations and unchurched individuals on the frontier turned to the evangelistic preachers of the Methodist and Baptist revivals for their religious identification. This same educational emphasis —on an educated membership who could read the Bible and the catechism—prompted the Presbyterians in the South to found a string of colleges and seminaries as they migrated westward and southwestward.

Presbyterians have historically been either townsfolk or, as in early Virginia and North Carolina, small farmers of owner-operated farms. From the late nineteenth century in the industrial areas we find large numbers of Presbyterians as mill owners and merchants, "gentlemen farmers," white-collar and professional people in towns, and educators. The heaviest Presbyterian concentration is in the regions of the Piedmont, East Tennessee, and East and Central Texas; and their socioeconomic status is the second highest among Southern Protestants, just below the Episcopalians. Their gatherings for family and church annual reunions are heavily focused on ancestors and/or church founders; and they rarely attend campmeetings except as guests or visitors with friends or family.

Baptist and Methodist churches in the rural and town South share in a frontier tradition associated with revival and camp-meeting preaching, with an emphasis on the personal salvation of those who repent. Country churches of these two denominations have many similarities, both being oriented to the fundamentalist style of preaching and biblical interpretation, and both being organized along lines of kin-based congregations. Their organizational style is associational, rather than the more hierarchical or more bureaucratic style of organization among their town brethren of the same denominational label. Both Methodist and Baptist country churches are likely to be set in the open country, to be surrounded by a graveyard, and to have long stone, wooden, or concrete tables near the church building for the holding of the reunions and homecomings. (This particular use of space is typical in only the earliest of Presbyterian churches. In the later settlements, the Presbyterian church was located in the town.)

The town versions of Methodist and Baptist churches

are divided along neighborhood lines and lines of socio-economic status. Separate congregations exist in the mill villages, in newer industrial neighborhoods, in older outlying neighborhoods of the town, and in the town center, where the ever-present "first church" is found. It is in the first church that one sees the prosperous business people and the clerks and white-collar workers of the Methodists and Baptists; it is in the outlying congregations, known as "chapels," that one finds tradespeople, workers, and mill employees. The major organizational distinction between town Methodists and town Baptists is in the hierarchical arrangement of Methodist Church government, in contrast to the egalitarian congregationalism of the Baptists, fiercely retaining their associational style even though they may have adopted aspects of bureaucracy. Some sociologists would like to place the Methodists above the Baptists on a scale of socioeconomic status, but this is highly variable from region to region in the South, and indeed will have great varia tion from one town to another. Baptist and Methodist family gatherings are based on loyalty to the living kin rather than to ancestors, and to outward "cousinship" rather than to lineal descent. Both Methodists and Baptists were early enthusiasts of the campmeeting; and today, while people of all denominations attend these gatherings, it is the Methodists and Baptists who act as the anchors and organizers of most contemporary camp-meeting grounds.

The Episcopalians have been ommitted from this analysis because in the studies we have conducted over the past six years we can find among Episcopalians little evidence of the specific patterns of religious familism being expressed in the kin-religious gatherings described here. Certainly Episcopalians in the South hold family get-togethers and go to church with their kinfolk on holidays; however, the explicit system of family, kin, and religious assemblies described here is not a central part of the tradition of most southern Episcopalian families. The Episcopal tradition in the South has been associated historically with the English church and with the plantation regions of the Virginia Tidewater and the South Carolina Low Country.

The kin-religious gatherings of the type discussed here are associated primarily with the Piedmont, the Shenandoah Valley, the Hill South, and the Cumberland Plateau. In addition to these areas, the gatherings are also held in parts of East Texas, where early Presbyterians migrated, and in northern Alabama and Mississippi among all three of the denominations studied.

My students and I attended and recorded information on various types of gatherings over a period of several years before arriving at categories that we believe approximate most nearly the categories agreed on by the participants themselves. Our observations were augmented by a survey questionnaire in which 205 people, theology students and members of an adult church school class, were asked to report on the gatherings they had attended. In addition, some students studied their own family reunion or a familiar church homecoming as a class project, and we analyzed these reports in comparison to the emerging categorical types that were coming from our systematic survey. At the same time, I added new information constantly from the reading of Southern literature—writers like Eudora Welty, William Faulkner, and Lillian Smith all refer to kin-religious gatherings by various names and describe them for various different subsegments of the Southern population.

The four gatherings selected as the most significant event types are, in fact, all related, in terms of their liturgical form and their cultural content, to the outdoor services described earlier. They exhibit a set of patterned regularities that can be summarized as follows:

1. Each one occurs annually, with the majority having a set repetitive day (for instance, the "second Sunday in July" or "the first Friday after the second Sunday in August").
2. The location of the gathering is a family homeplace in the country, a family cemetery, or a church. Most frequently the event itself is held outdoors, while segments of it may be inside a house or church building.
3. The participants in each conceptualize their relationship as that of "the descendants of a common ancestor," either a real person of the great-grandparent generation or a set of church founders now resting in the graveyard.
4. Each type contains within its composition a complex of symbols representing the family and the church. These include the common meal, the shared prayers and sermon of a church homecoming, the graves of the ancestors, and various material items of significance to the family or church (for example family Bible, pictures or memorabilia, church historical records, and memorial gift items.)

An additional feature which has both behavioral and symbolic aspects is that of the centrality of the mother in the linkage between generations and in the organizational components of ongoing family and religious life. The role of mother as family ritual specialist is significant because the pattern and structure of family ritual provides a learning situation for children to absorb cultural meanings and values. The mother is the liturgist in this complicated set of liturgical forms. Her knowledge of the appropriate order of a ceremonial meal and its material culture is crucial. This material culture includes the proper tablecloth, the appropriate silver or eating utensils, china or "everyday dishes" as the occasion demands, as well as the right foods for each separate occasion. The mother is also a liturgical specialist in the social ordering of the universe of each event; that is, she knows the right seating arrangement, the correct order of serving people, whom to assign the task of carving and of offering the blessing of the meal. In the extended family gatherings, the mother is responsible for the advance notices, for arranging for and cleaning the house or campmeeting cottage, seeing that everyone has lodging for overnight visits, and planning for the care and feeding of the assembled family over an extended period of time. The intriguing question of how daughters learn these unwritten rules and regulations of family liturgy is at the heart of the inquiry into the learning of culture.[5]

The mother serves as the head of her own three-generation family and at the same time is one of several daughters and sons who form a sibling group under a grandmother's three-generation or four-generation family group. The link between mothers and daughters is strengthened summer after summer in the custom of kin-visiting by a married daughter with her own children in the home of the grandmother. In this way the daughter's children become closely associated through recurrent coparticipation in this visiting pattern, while the children of the brothers are visiting at the home of their own mother's mother. Furthermore, our data indicate that a tendency exists among Southern families to participate with a higher frequency in the extended family gatherings on the mother's side of the family than on the father's side, if the prestige of both families is equal. Anthropologists refer to this type of kinship trend as a *matrilineal* tendency.

The Family Dinner
The first gathering to be discussed is the family dinner. This occurs as a family universal in the American South in every region and among both town and country people of all white Protestant groups. The family dinner may vary in form from one group to another, but it follows certain liturgical regularities.

A family dinner is a shared meal taken at the home of the parents of grown children who now live elsewhere. The dinner is an occasion for all the children and grandchildren of a couple to reassemble for a ceremonial meal, and for renewal of kinship ties. Children who have grown and moved away return home on a regular basis with their own spouses and children to visit their parents and grandparents, to celebrate holidays, and to join in a special meal of this kind. Any one family dinner will begin with the arrival of the first son or daughter and their family from afar and will develop through the gradual assembling and visiting of each of the nuclear families. The shared meal may be a Sunday dinner or a holiday meal, as Christmas or Thanksgiving. After the meal, adult women visit and gossip, children play outdoor games or sports, and the men watch sports on television. If family members live at a distance, they may stay overnight before or after the day of the dinner, possibly visiting other relatives who live nearby.

All of the respondents in our study reported having taken part in one or more of these recurring family dinners. They occur at almost every American holiday time, but each family has a set day or days that is preferred for the expected gathering. The most popular by far is Christmas Day, with Thanksgiving Day next. Easter and Mother's Day drop far behind in popularity. Other days reported include Father's Day and Grandmother's birthday.

The dinner is most frequently held at the grandmother's house, but the place will vary with the age of the family and with that particular family's place in its life cycle. If grandmother is too old to manage the crowd, the place will be shifted to the home of a daughter in the next generation who lives in the same vicinity as the grandmother. This shifting pattern represents a flexibility in the domestic cycle to accommodate the needs created by daughters and sons moving long distances from the "home place." Three-fourths of our respondents reported the place of the family dinner as the home of the oldest living female in the three-generation family. By the time of grandmother's death, if she lives to old age, her daughters will be eligible for the establishment of their own separate matri-centered, three-generation family dinners, and the family gathering will break into separate segments at these holiday times.

Young couples find it difficult to choose between attending the family dinner of the husband or the wife. Christmas time, one of the most difficult to decide, is often divided between the two families, or it is alternated. Distance is an important determinant of who comes to family dinners. When all factors are equal and both sets of grandparents are living, the couple must work out their own set of rules. The resulting solutions often informally favor the selection of the wife's family over the husband's, again expressing the matrilineal tendency mentioned earlier. Family conflict sometimes erupts over this item, with the husband's mother as the injured party blaming the errant daughter-in-law for taking away a son during a family ceremonial time. Families attempt to adjust for conflicts of this kind by compromising and having one family shift its ceremonial dinner to a different day or another holiday period. This becomes extremely difficult when long-standing tradition dictates a certain set recurring day over the family's history. The issue is one which presents a seemingly irreconcilable dilemma for each young couple to solve in their own specific way.

The order of action internal to the family dinner expresses a combination of kinship and religious themes. Families who may not always attend church are more likely to go to church together at this time, especially for Christmas Eve, Thanksgiving Day, or Easter. Even if the family does not regularly practice "saying the blessing" over daily meals, "the blessing" takes on a regular and prescribed place at the beginning of the ceremonial meal. In some families the father or grandfather reads a portion of Scripture during the Christmas dinner blessing period, and during the Thanksgiving blessing he will ceremonially state all the things for which the family should be thankful. Regarding the regular religious life of participants, family dinners are times for parents to ask the married children where they are attending church and whether the grandchildren are being taken to Sunday School. Some informants report that this informal pressure has been the cause of many disagreements and has resulted in tears or uncomfortable silences some time during the day or weekend of the family gathering.

The family dinner involves a specific liturgical form, unwritten but rigid in its proper order and execution. As the culture specialist and "folk liturgist," the mother is in charge of this significant event in the ritual life of the private domain. As does a dinner in a kosher Jewish household, a well-ordered traditional Protestant family dinner requires complicated internal sets of actions for the celebration to be successful. When the mother refers to "making Christmas," "having Christmas at our house," or "coming home for Christmas," she is alluding to an extended preparation for the ritual celebration. The execution of this event will mean months of pre-planning, writing to the children, assembling gifts and food, baking the fruitcake and other ceremonial delicacies on schedule so they will age properly or not spoil, cleaning the house and getting extra bedding ready, ironing tablecloths and napkins, decorating for the holiday season, and, finally, preparing the ceremonial meal itself. In this final phase, if she is fortunate, she will have the assistance of any daughters who live nearby or who have arrived a few days early. In reenacting all these preparations through the years, daughters and grand-daughters are taught in subtle ways the fine arts of being a ritual specialist.

Family dinners are a composite of social relations and cultural meanings. We find a family, as a concrete social action, more extended than the isolated nuclear household. We find symbolic expressions of family loyalty, common heritage, and traditional religious beliefs and values. These same social actions and cultural meanings are also seen in other types of kin-religious gatherings, where several—sometimes many—of the three-generation families come together.

The family reunion as an annual ceremonial event may in fact have begun as the three-generation family dinner of a large family who later were scattered by moves into cities. After the establishment of their own households and the extension of their numbers of children, these separate nuclear families may have begun the practice of regathering annually with their offspring at the family homeplace or at a suitable substitute for grandmother's house.

The Family Reunion

The family reunion is a gathering that includes all the sons and daughters of one couple, sometimes deceased, and all their children and grandchildren. If this original couple is several generations removed, the relationship will be expressed as "all the descendants of " a particular ancestor or an ancestral couple. Those who identify themselves as among this set of descendants gather each year at some rural spot for a day-long celebration of kin-visiting, feasting on traditional Southern foods, and enjoyment of games and fun with cousins, aunts, and uncles.[6]

In the event that a couple who married in the mid-1800s had nine children, all of whom married and reproduced, by 1977 the eligible reunion participants would be in the hundreds. Reunions did not take on great popularity in the South until about fifty to seventy years ago. This can partly be explained by the great scattering of individuals off the family land in the late nineteenth and early twentieth centuries. If families lived near one another, or if they left the farm and emigrated too far to return, the day-to-day association did not require a reunion. Those nearby associated with their aunts, uncles, and cousins in the ongoing routines of town and country life.

Family reunions, in our study, were found to occur throughout the year, but by far the majority are held in late spring and summer. They may also be held on religious holidays or on the birthday of an elderly or a deceased grandmother. The most often reported spot is grandmother's house or a family home, but reunions can also be held at camp-meeting grounds, rural churches, or town community buildings. There is a clear distinction between a family dinner and a family reunion. A family reunion includes all the "greater family" beyond one three-generation group and has its own specific liturgical regularities.

The activity of a family reunion begins two or three days before the event itself, with those members who are local residents making preparations. Of course there has been preplanning, as in a family dinner, which includes similar kinds of preparations of the house or picnic grounds and a general notification of the family members. Formal invitations or notices need not be sent for most reunions, which recur on the same day each summer—for instance, on the second Sunday in June. Activities of local residents during the reunion week may include the setting up of long tables outside a church or campmeeting or providing folding tables and chairs on grandmother's front lawn, preparing large tubs of ice for tea and cold drinks, and making arrangements for the cookout or barbecue on the night before the reunion day. If the celebration is to be on a Sunday, participants begin arriving on Friday or Saturday to visit with kinfolks who live nearby.

The day before the reunion, usually Saturday, is filled with informal kin-visiting and the final preparations of food. Many families hold a hamburger cookout or informal barbecue on this night for early arrivals. Other families hold special meetings on Saturday for the discussion of family business, for example the joint ownership of land or investments; some hold a special program, and many go together to visit the graveyard where the family ancestors are buried.

On the day of the reunion, participants begin to gather at the site in the late morning. Informal conversation among the women and men (separately) begins as arrivals speed up. Teen-agers stand and chat with cousins, and children run about playing games of tag. As the morning progresses, the women lay the food out on the long row of tables. The traditional dishes of fried chicken, potato salad, deviled eggs, summer vegetables, pies, and cakes appear, each one the specialty of one of the mothers who attends. The blessing is given by an older male family member—preferably one who is a minister—or by a local minister invited for the occasion. The participants file along the common table, filling their plates with the colorful and appetizing dishes they remember from other years and other family reunion feasts.

During the meal, families sit together in three-generation groupings to eat and talk. Slowly, after the meal, the three-generation families disperse again into groups according to age and sex. While the men and younger couples play softball, touch football, or other games, the women chat, care for children, and, later, clear away the tables. Among these women, and among the older men, the afternoon includes serious talk about the worries over absent family members, concern for the ill or for the recently widowed, along with items of family history and church policy.

In the late afternoon, as the middle-aged women begin to clean up the tables and pack away their leftover food, children are instructed to file by to pay homage to their grandmothers and great-aunts before the group slowly disbands and returns to their everyday residences in city and town.

In the family reunion we find that the assemblage of a large extended family is based on descent from common ancestors. This group is composed of a number of three-generation units which can trace their descent to the same grandparents or great-grandparents. Descent is traced through both males and females. Presbyterian families have a greater tendency to hold reunions in honor of ancestors from the eighteenth or early nineteenth centuries, a period of heavy Presbyterian settlement in the South, which results in reunions that are genuinely ancestor-focused rather than focused on the living kin group. The structure is the same, however, among Methodists and Baptists, except that their lineal emphasis is not as great. Their reunions focus instead on lateral ties with all the cousins whose parents and grandparents were children of a couple in the more recent past.

The emphasis on deceased family members and on early ancestors is seen in the activities concerning the graveyard that are associated with reunions. In addition to the visits to the ancestral burial place, some families take the day before the reunion to clean or to place flowers on the graves of the family dead. A few families report holding the reunion itself in an old family graveyard on the grounds of the ancestral homeplace. The graveyard also plays an important part in the symbolic expressions of the other kin-religious gatherings discussed here.

The name or label used for the total family, living and dead, varies from family to family. Some refer to "the larger family," others to "the whole family," "the Russell clan," or "the greater family." This last term is frequently used and seems to refer to all the members, both those present and absent, who would ideally be included in the perfectly formed reunion. Often simply "the family" is used to refer to this ideal set. When participants speak of "the family" or of "our family," they are seldom referring only to the nuclear version of the family, or even to the three-generation family, but to the wider group of kin who assemble for the reunion.

The two events cited so far, the family dinner and the family reunion, are based on kinship and family loyalty with certain religious overtones. The religious nature of the family reunion was stated in the negative response of one informant who was asked if he attended reunions. His answer was "My family doesn't do that sort of thing, because they are not religious." The family reunion holds crucial religious significance, as demonstrated by this quotation from a letter written by an informant in response to the question "Why do you attend the family reunion year after year?" It is a testimony of an older brother in a family whose reunion is a classic example of the type we have presented.

> Family reunions always have a spiritual quality because of the love that brought the family together in the first instance. The fact of life and death, careers, labor and love, ambitions and aspirations, are brought together in a brief get-together in the mystery of human life which evokes faith and trust and assists in the development of conviction and confidence. . . . There are prayers and memorials, fun and frolic, food and fellowship, music and singing, and all with the strong arms of a trust which deals with a vastness of time and space with assurance, saying: "Lord, thou hast been our dwelling place in all generations . . ."[7]

The next two event categories presented will be those based on religious loyalties, with strong and important family and kin aspects.

The Church Homecoming
The church homecoming fits well into the model provided for a family reunion in that it offers an annual format for gathering together all the "sons and daughters of the congregation." In the homecoming assembly on one Sunday every summer, a rural congregation welcomes back all the members and former members who

have moved away into the cities but whose religious ties from childhood and whose family historical ties belong to a particular rural church. Other labels for the same event include church reunion, May meeting or October meeting, Decoration Day (found predominantly among rural Baptists, especially in the Piedmont), Founders' Day, and Graveyard Association Day. In Appalachia a similar event is known as a "graveyard reunion." These labels represent minor variations on a basic pattern; all of the above were classified together due to their structural regularities.

Church homecomings are held most frequently in the summer months, but they may occur at any time of the year. Over eighty percent of those reported in this study were held in late spring and summer months, with the older rural churches holding homecomings almost exclusively in the spring to summer period. Urban and town churches hold homecomings at other times, and they tend to be indoor rather than outdoor occasions.

Rural church homecomings are held without exception outdoors on the grounds of the church or in the graveyard adjoining church grounds. The gathering is held on a recurring Sunday, and during the morning worship service the announcements, introductions, prayers, and sermon deal with the homecoming themes —the church as a sacred place with a history and ancestry, the locality of the church community and its history, and the hardy pioneers who founded the church. Founders and ancestors play an important part in the homecomings, both as individual people to be honored and admired and as part of the great "family of faith," which includes the attenders on that day and all the members of the church family who are now resting in the graveyard of the congregation.

The order of activity at a church homecoming is closely parallel to that of the family reunion, except that it is interrupted at 11:00 A.M. by a worship service. During the sermon, often delivered by an older revered minister who is a "son of the congregation," historic themes are emphasized and anecdotes refer to the church's past. During announcements, returning families are noted and honored. Following the service everyone files out onto the grounds where, as in the reunion, long tables have been set up. In one North Georgia rural congregation Sunday School is not held on homecoming Sunday, so that the women can stay at home and cook. The results of this endeavor appear following the worship service, again with individual specialties in abundance. The food, the order of action, and the seating pattern resemble so closely that of a family reunion that the aforementioned anthropologist from Mars might classify them as the same event. Families sit together at separate tables, then they break off into age-graded groups for visiting. Large segments of several kin groups make up the central participating group of this event, to the extent that at one homecoming we were told: "This is just like a reunion of the King family."

At the homecoming, however, the King family—or whatever major kin group dominates the church—is joined by other large families of three and four generations, who have all come together for this occasion. The loyalty here is lodged not primarily in the family and kin but in the locale of this particular congregational community. The separate families are joined by the social glue of shared religious beliefs and a long history of common ritual observances. Although many are also actually distantly related through intermarriage of their ancestors, the relationship emphasized is through the church itself. A sense of continuity is engendered in these ways among a transgenerational, intrafamily, religious community.

The church homecoming serves as a reunion of a number of families who are not related by blood descent, as in the family reunion, but by common religious descent reinforced by ties of kinship. The congregation itself, rooted in a particular locality over time, becomes a central focus for unification of a group of people with a shared cultural identity. This type of religious-cultural identity reinforced by kin ties is also seen in the final type of gathering to be described—that of the campmeeting.

The Campmeeting

The campmeeting is frequently referred to in the literature on the religion of the South as having been an important historical form typical of the Great Revival Period on the American frontier.[8] Few writers have recognized the presence and power of the campmeeting as a contemporary social form which continues to serve as a focus for religious expression among large numbers of people in the 1970s. Campmeetings abound in the North Georgia Piedmont and in East Tennessee; and a few are found in the Piedmont region of South Carolina and North Carolina. In this study, thirty-five campmeetings were analyzed, most of which were in North Georgia. The term "campmeeting" refers not only to the gathering and the associated religious services but also to the grounds and to the buildings where the gathering is held.

The central building is known as the "arbor." This label presumably derives from the early campmeeting days when a covering of small trees and "brush" was constructed for the preacher to use as a shelter while he preached. Early references to campmeetings sometimes call them "brush-arbor meetings." The preaching services take place under the arbor twice daily for the week of campmeeting. Inside the arbor are the lines of pews or wooden benches, a dirt floor often covered with wood shavings or pinestraw, and a raised platform for the preacher and the choir.

The campground cabins are individually owned by separate three-generation families and greater families, whose members are free to stay in the cabin during the week of services. The cabins are spoken of by participants as "tents," and the practice of moving in for the week is known as "tenting."

Tenting famlies in any one campground can trace their history of participation for many generations, some as far back as the 1840s when the majority of the camp-meeting grounds in North Georgia were founded. The families who have attended campmeetings together over long periods are also interrelated through ties of kinship, and many older couples report having courted their spouses during campmeeting season.

The tent-owning families begin arriving early in the appointed week. Participants in campmeetings generally come from the immediate surrounding area, the majority of attenders in our study live within 100 miles of the campmeeting ground. Even so, they bring their belongings and stay over in the family tent for the entire week if possible.

Many families who attend campmeeting also hold family reunions; some of these hold their reunions at the campmeeting grounds on a particular Sunday in the summer before the campmeeting season. Even though the reunion may be held at the site of the campmeeting, it is clearly a separate event. At the reunion a group of blood descendants honor one common ancestor or an ancestral couple, while at the campmeeting the members of the kin group gather with other kin groups to celebrate a common religious affiliation with one rural locale and one style of revivalistic worship and preaching.

When asked to recount the sequence of activities at a campmeeting, one informant answered: "We do the same things we do at the family reunion except we do it all week long and have religious services too." Services are held as often as four times a day or as few as two. One may be aimed at the younger members, who also have special activities planned for them by the college youth leaders chosen by the campmeeting association. At one campmeeting where the arbor is referred to as the "tabernacle," an Old Testament designation, the youth building is known as the "nab-r-tackle" in good humored fashion.

All the family attends the evening service together. The fathers who had driven to their work in town or to their farms in the early morning will have returned by late afternoon for supper and for the service. A special preacher is invited to give the sermons through the week, frequently a minister of a prominent church in a nearby city or a minister noted for his speaking ability at these occasions. In the twilight the old Gospel songs ring out over the countryside, the sermon follows, and then the meeting is ended with the altar call or "the invitation." Those who have been moved by the sermon are invited to come forward to the altar, renew their commitment, and rededicate their lives to the Christian faith. This altar call is different from the call forward at conversion revivals, where the goal is to get sinners to repent and join the church. These people are long-standing members of local churches and have come forward many times during campmeetings to renew their vows and promise their obedience. The altar call is an essential element in the liturgical form of the campmeeting service, the final act before the benediction is pronounced.

After the service the families drift back to their respective tents for coffee and more visiting until time to bed
down for the night in the dormitory-style sleeping lofts
of the rustic cabins.

Many families who traditionally attend the meetings
plan their summer vacation to coincide with the dates of
the campmeeting. Campmeetings are held without exception in the summer, with three-fourths of those studied held in August. This timing fits neatly with the
Southern agricultural cycle, which allows a lull in farm-
ing activity during August "after the crops are laid by"
and before the harvest period. Even though the participants may be rural people, either farmers or small-town
dwellers, great emphasis is placed on getting away from
daily work routines and withdrawing into the woods to
be close to nature. The drawing apart from everyday
work activity represents a separation into a religious
sphere of activity for the purpose of being renewed. The
renewal is apparently accomplished by listening to the
inspiring messages of the preacher and by sharing this
experience with their kinfolk and friends. Campmeetings are not aimed at the conversion of the unsaved but
at providing the saved with a recurrent ritual of regener-
ation.

The campmeeting is structurally similar to the church
homecoming in that we see in both a reassembling of a
scattered network of people joined for religious activities
who are also tied together by kinship. In addition, both
provide a locus for the symbolic statement of culturally
defined religious beliefs and values. The differences between these two religious gatherings center in the connection of the participants to the local congregation. In
the homecoming some, in fact, attend that church regularly on Sunday mornings. At the campmeeting, in contrast, participants are connected to this locale for only

one week during the summer and there are no recurrent continuing weekly participators. There is some evidence that church homecomings are more a part of institution-alized, officially sanctioned, formal denominational life, especially among the Presbyterians and Methodists. While the church bureaucracy and the ecclesiastical hier-archy take part in homecomings, the institutional coor-dinating bodies and the more institutionally tied "high churches" of these two denominations look with mild disdain at the people whose cycle of participation in-cludes a "campmeeting religion."

Campmeetings, nevertheless, are important religious and kinship events in the rural and town-dwelling South, and they draw numerous urban residents out into the countryside each summer. They provide a locus for the expression of culture in a setting of transfamilial community and for the symbolic statement of a cultural tradition that embodies the crucial elements of religious familism.

Religious Familism and the Culture of Southern Protestants

The description given here of the pattern and process of kin-religious gatherings illustrates the ways in which the phenomenon of religious familism is expressed among the white Anglo-Saxon Protestants who comprise the main component of the population of the American South. In the recurrent regathering of three and four generation families for dinners, reunions, homecomings, and campmeetings, scattered people annually renew their ties to the church and the clan of the historical tradition and of their cultural heritage. The gatherings are not themselves traditional forms, "folkways," or merely remnants of a past way of life. They are new creations of the people whose communities and families have been radically altered by waves of land-use change, urbanization, and industrialization, giving rise to the population shifts of the past hundred years. In the kin-religious gatherings we see a response to these shifts, an establishment of a locus for assemblage and for restatement symbolically of cultural themes of family and church.

In the regularity and repetitiveness of the internal activities and expected behaviors of each of the events, there is a patterned liturgical form that is understood by the participants as the proper way to carry out the event in question. The rules are as rigidly regular as if they were recorded in the Book of Common Worship or in a guide to the Methodist liturgy. The structure of the events remains constant from year to year, while the actual personnel changes.

We see also in the celebration of the ceremonies a complex of symbols associated with family and church. These include family land, house, or properties, as well as heirlooms associated with certain ancestors. Examples of symbolic heirlooms are the great-grandfather's sword, carried in the War Between the States, or grandmother's bed, where all the aunts and uncles were born. The family plot in the church graveyard becomes an important symbolic statement of the continuity of the family of faith, as does the family tent or cabin at the campmeeting grounds. The permanent long tables that stand outside each rural church or campmeeting arbor form the symbolic focus of the communal meal, the equivalent of the Lord's table in the indoor service of Eucharist, or Holy Communion. The tables when laden with food become the sacramental altar for the "communion of the saints," a deeply embedded Protestant idea in which the people of the church are joined in fellowship.

The oral tradition accompanying the events is one of family histories and the history of the locale of the gathering. Songs retell the glories of being a member of the community of faith; sermons and other formal rhetoric underline the rewards of the godly life and the pursuit of virtue and truth.

In their participation in this complicated set of interlocking symbolic actions and activities, thousands of town and urban dwellers bring into being each year the central cultural themes of Southern Protestantism. Through these activities too, they provide a ritual locale in which aspects of this culture are learned by successive waves of the young.

These gatherings give us, as observers and as participants, an opportunity to understand the essential elements in the structure of a culture—laid out in the form of action, process, meaning, and values—and the way these elements are translated into liturgical pattern and process. The gatherings form a crucial locus for a people to restate repetitively their cultural reality and to insure that this reality will become a part of the lives of their children.

The cyclical rituals, or calendrical ceremonies, of families and of churches provide one important means of culture learning in liturgical context. Another important liturgical context within which learning takes place is that of the life-crisis ritual, treated next in the exploration of baptism as a family liturgy.

· 3 ·

Baptism:
A Life-Crisis Liturgy[1]

Baptism is a ceremony which carries strong cultural and social meanings in addition to its stated religious and symbolic ones. As educated Christians, we are often more familiar with the religious significance of baptism and other ceremonies than we are aware of the social usefulness of these events in the organization of a human community. In this chapter I will look at baptism in its social and cultural context, as a life-crisis ceremony, or rite of passage. As a rite of passage, baptism serves three important functions in the life cycle of individuals and communities. One of these is the incorporation of a new infant member into an existing social group. Another is the initiation of the infant's parents into a new social status—that of parents. A third is to provide a ceremonial gathering place for the parents, grandparents, and close friends to affirm the infant and the parents and to accept partial responsibility for assisting in the tasks of child rearing. Before we take a closer look at these three separate but complementary social functions of baptism, it is necessary to examine the meaning and structure of rites of passage as they have been identified and analyzed for a wide range of human communities.

Rite of passage is the name assigned to ceremonies marking abrupt shifts in human social relations resulting from changes in position within the life cycle. Anthropologist Arnold van Gennep first defined and described rites of passage after he had noted from his readings and research on human societies that in every culture these marking ceremonies existed.[2] Individuals move in sequence over time from one state in expected relations with other people into another state. Within the human life cycle, in other words, there is a process of movement from unborn infant to infant, infant to child, child into puberty and then into adulthood, and so on. At each change in state there is a change in expected behaviors which that individual must accept; for example, an adult is expected to behave differently from a child. These shifts in behavior and in group relations are accompanied by ritual and symbolic celebrations of the community or the congregation. In the Jewish tradition, for instance, the Bar Mitzvah at age thirteen marks the social transition of a young man from boyhood into manhood, even though his complete physical growth will not be reached for several years. After this ceremony a young man is eligible to take part in men's activities of the synagogue, and he is no longer expected to behave like a child. The major shifts in behavior accompanying these processes of change are designated as "life crises" because there is a crisis of changed social relations. The individual has passed a crisis when she or he learns to fit appropriately into the new situation. The group also undergoes a crisis whenever one of its members enters, grows into adulthood, or dies.

Ceremonies also mark social transitions that are not strictly tied to individual growth. In the marriage ceremony, for instance, two individuals who have been treated as single persons socially are transformed within a set ritual from singles into a couple. Ceremonies of initiation into sororities and fraternities mark a transition from pledge into sister or brother. Ordination ceremonies mark a social transition from layman or laywoman into priest or minister. In short, the entire social structure of a society could conceivably be viewed as an interlocking set of life cycles in process from one stage into another. Moving states of each life cycle are set into counterpoint with other states to form the fabric of ongoing human cultural organization.

Because the life crises are integral to understanding human communities, rituals and ceremonies accompanying them have been a focus of study by anthropologists. The internal structure of the ceremonies themselves has been an object of study for those interested in unraveling the threads of ritual language and behavior in relation to everyday life activities.

Each ceremony seems to share certain characteristics with every other life-crisis ceremony. Within each ceremony there are three phases: (1) separation, (2) transition, and (3) incorporation. In the first phase, the participant who is being moved into a new state of being is separated symbolically from her or his old state of life. This separation is seen most extensively in the weeks or months of withdrawal into the wilderness that is required of young people in many of the world's tribal societies before returning to undergo the rites of passage into adulthood. During this period of separation they are trained by older men or older women in the skills of adult life in that village and often are subjected to a series of ordeals or obstacles which they must overcome in order to be eligible for adult privilege. Many writers have come to compare this elaborate separation-training-ordeal endurance period to our own long months or years of separation in training institutions for specialized professions. The comparison also applies to the months of pregnancy during which a woman gradually begins withdrawing from her former way of life and work; in earlier times she was expected to separate herself completely from social interaction during her entire pregnancy. During her first pregnancy, at least, she was undergoing a period of separation before her shift in status from an individual woman to a mother.

The second stage of a rite of passage is the middle, transitional, stage, in which the participant is in flux— "betwixt and between," as noted by anthropologist Victor Turner.[3] It is in this period, which Turner calls "liminality," that the core symbolic actions and words serve to transport the individual and the group into a state of highly aroused consciousness in which they are intensely aware and share a heightened expectedness. Going through a service of baptism or a marriage service together with one's family or friends produces a kind of commonality of religious experience that most people have felt at one time or another, although the feeling is often difficult to explain. This is certainly true of the shared feeling of common experience among those who have undergone a fraternity initiation in which ordeals were successfully performed and obstacles surmounted.

Compared to other phases in the ceremony, the transition phase is often the longest phase of the ritual event. It constitutes, for instance, a major portion of our contemporary wedding service. At this stage the bride and groom are in a state of being neither married nor unmarried; they have been given over by their parents and have proceeded onto the sacred portion of the chancel, but until the priest pronounces that they are husband and wife they remain in liminality, neither here nor there. It is during this middle segment of a baptism ceremony that the godparent or minister will often take the baby into his or her arms, symbolizing spatially the transition from an unbaptized condition into a new position as a member of a church community.

The third stage in all rites of passage is the stage of

incorporation. During this final stage the individual is received into the new group into which he or she has passed. The well-wishers stand outside the church or in the reception hall to receive the bride and groom into their new state, as family and friends celebrate the baptized infant with gifts and good wishes.

One way of analyzing ritual processes is to focus only on the portion of events contained by the ceremonial service itself. In our society that would include the part that takes place within the church during the service. A broader view of ritual and of life-crisis transitions focuses on the total process of movement from beginning to end within the interacting social group as the field of analysis. For instance, in this broader view one would look not only at the baptism ceremony and what it explicitly does symbolically but at the transition of the parents beginning from the time they learn of the pregnancy through the end of the baptism, including all the rituals surrounding the pregnancy and the birth.

Using this total process model for analysis we see that baptism fits into a whole sequence of events forming the social transition for both infant and parents to a new social state. Because the infant is officially emphasized in ecclesiastical tradition as the individual who is being acted upon during baptism, we will begin with the social context of baptism as a ceremony for the incorporation of a new member into an already existing group.

Baptism as Incorporation

The event of birth is, like that of death, a natural happening which has evoked various cultural explanations. In the human group, birth is experienced as both a natural and a mysterious event. For us, the natural, biological development of the fetus and its entry into the outside world through the mother's birth canal have all been explained by modern obstetrics. The mysterious elements are assigned to philosophers to explain in their philosophies of human nature, and to theologians to explain in their religious systems and theologies. There seems to be inherent in the human species a need to categorize and attempt explanations for seemingly unexplainable events.

Birth is mysterious partly because it introduces a new human being into a group that was already getting along in a well balanced way. A new person is thrust suddenly into the social group—an intrusion that must be explained and in some way fitted into the cognitive system which that culture has developed for categorizing human events and explaining the relationship between humans and the natural world.

Christians have explained this relationship in part by assigning the birth of a new human being to the realm of God's activity as Creator. The new member of the social unit is categorized as a creature, a "child of God," and as such it is immediately fitted into existing explanation systems for reality.

In modern complex society, a child is born into two worlds: the public, civil realm and the private, kin-religious one. In the act of giving a name to a child on the rolls of both county and church, the parents further transform this nonperson into an individual with both a civil and a religious identity. By taking the child to be baptized they are assigning a name to the child in the eyes of God, thus creating a religious-cultural identity to go along with the civil one. While the civil realm will claim the child as he or she is enrolled on the county record, in the social security records, and tax rolls, the religious-cultural realm will claim the same citizen as a member of a separate kingdom belonging to God and the people of God.

The ceremony of baptism enacts this transformation

symbolically within the religious realm. A life-crisis event is being experienced by the infant in its very enrollment as a new citizen and as a citizen of the religious realm. The transition from having been a nonperson into now being an active social person is symbolically accomplished for the civil realm at the time of delivery, with its attendant rituals of cleaning, dressing, washing, taking footprints, tagging with a bracelet, and making out a birth certificate. The same transition into personhood within a faith community is symbolically accomplished within the ceremony of baptism. At this time the infant is ritually separated from the status of the nonmember, moved through a transitional phase of prayers, blessings, symbolic use of water, and finally incorporated into the Christian community through being "baptized in the name of the Father, the Son, and the Holy Spirit." The infant's name is called at this time—which in some traditions has been termed a "naming ceremony" or a "christening." The name of the infant is thus placed symbolically within the circle of the family of the already named believers.

Baptism as Initiation of Parents

In addition to its social function in marking the incorporation of a new infant into a community, baptism also carries an important function in the initiation of new parents. The baptism of the couple's first infant is the most significant in this sense, due to the fact that in our society the arrival of a first baby is truly a life crisis of major proportions. Until this time a couple is allowed to remain in the "honeymoon" period of early marriage, concentrating on their personal relationship and their individual careers or interests. Even their friends and social involvements remain similar to those of single young adults, and they are free to take part at their own choice in clubs, parties, trips, or quiet evenings at home. The birth of the first baby brings about a sudden shift in all these activities. Now it becomes necessary to take along the nursing infant or to get a baby-sitter when the couple plans the simplest outing. Quiet evenings at home are interrupted by feeding, fussing, colic, teething, as tired parents attempt to adjust to the requirements of their new role.

The life crisis is made even more traumatic in many cases by the gap in experience of young expectant parents who were not reared in the context of large families with many babies. In our small nuclear families, with cousins living far away, a young couple might enter the formidable period of parenthood without having ever held a newborn infant or cared for a toddler brother, sister, or cousin. Young people learn their child-care skills most often through a combination of Dr. Spock and trial-and-error. Classes at hospitals and at the Red Cross have emerged to fill the vacuum in preparation for child care, but unfortunately many of these are too brief to meet the many needs of new parents.

Initiation rituals for parenthood begin almost immediately after the woman learns she is pregnant and continue throughout the infant's early months. Central in the prenatal period of ceremonial preparation for the approaching life-crisis event is the obstetrician's office or the obstetrical clinic. Within the context of modern medicine and health care the young woman begins her gradual ceremonial shift in status from individual to mother, surrounded by the recurrent rituals of monthly checkups, medical advice, preparatory exercises, diet, and reading.

Medical rituals surrounding the big change are accompanied by other forms of ceremonies and gatherings in which friends and family assemble for congratulations and to bring gifts—the perennial baby shower, often held near the time when the woman shifts into the new pattern of home-bound activity, having left her job at the office or having taken a temporary leave from her professional life.

The period of separation of the mother from her previous normal activities has fortunately been gradually shortening, and often her separation into seclusion lasts only during the labor and delivery itself. In another very fortunate move, medical centers are increasingly aware of the value of having the father accompany the mother in the labor suite and assist by coaching her on exercises and breathing to ease the delivery. In this way the father is being ceremonially separated along with the mother, and his own initiation into parenthood is marked more significantly than it was in the past.

While in the hospital, the mother remains in a state of semiliminality. She is still in transition into motherhood, symbolized by the separation in most hospitals of the baby into a baby nursery. She is not allowed to care for her own infant until the final incorporation is accomplished through going home with her infant in her own arms.

Both members of the couple are welcomed into the social state of parents by hospital attendants, visiting nurses, family, friends, insurance salespeople, newspaper announcements, cards, letters, gifts, and flowers. The church has traditionally played a role in this welcoming when the priest or pastor has come to call on the new parents. Prayers are offered for a safe delivery and for the health of the mother and infant.

In the Christian tradition, the mother is believed to be an assistant in the process of creation, but often a folk belief persists that assigns birth to uncleanliness and makes women the victims of practices and unstated fears regarding ritual pollution. In the Roman Catholic and Episcopal traditions a special home ceremony was once customary, called "The Churching of Women," which resembled in many ways some of the ritual cleansing ceremonials practiced by tribal peoples after the birth of an infant.

The goal of ceremonies, services, and prayers surrounding childbirth should be to affirm and support the young mother and to celebrate all the processes of labor, delivery, and breast-feeding as good, clean, and positive aspects of her personhood and of her participation in the ongoing life of the community.

The initiation into parenthood in our society and its subcultural traditions is sporadic and in many instances incomplete. Couples living in cities, away from their parents or other kin, have scanty support for this awesome new task they have assumed. Doctors, ministers, and priests are most often males who are unable to relate personally to the experience of giving birth and caring for infants; the young woman is left with little encouragement from those her society tells her should be experts.

Baptism acts to augment the slender support base by providing a locus of assemblage for family and friends who fill in this encouragement gap. Even though grandmother and the female kin may live hundreds of miles away, they attempt to come to the infant's baptism, symbolizing spatially their continued support and assistance. Within the enactment of the ceremony all the participants take on a segment of the responsibility for this child's upbringing, thus easing considerably the burden of the overburdened new parents. In the words and prayers, and in the questions and answers exchanged by the parents and the priest or minister, the parents are initiated into the role of parents within their faith community. They have already been incorporated into the civil status of parents by the hospital and the government. Now they are ceremonially transferred into the status of parents within the religious community. Their place in the ongoing tradition is recognized, and their task is placed in the context of a cooperating social group who are willing to share wisdom and aid. Their place as assistants in creation is now overlaid by their place in transmitting a cultural heritage, teaching the child the ways of the people—"raising the child in the nurture and admonition of the Lord," as stated in one tradition. The parents and the grandparents are initiated into their new roles in the ongoing process of cultural transmission.

Baptism as Celebration

We have seen the ways in which baptism serves as a rite of passage for the infant in his or her incorporation into a religious community. We have also examined the function of baptism as a rite of passage for the new parents as they become initiated into a new social position with new responsibilities. There is a third social function served by baptism in relation to the assembled group of celebrants, and in a wider sense to the entire congregation even though it may not be present at the service itself. In the act of performing a baptism, the priest or minister of the congregation is symbolizing the inclusion of a new member for whom the total congregation becomes partially responsible, just as in the civil realm the state is ultimately responsible for the well-being of all its citizens.

In every Christian tradition the arrival of infants is in some way noted, even if infant baptism is not practiced. This is significant, because it tells us that the entire group experiences a change in its group life when another unit is added. In the Southern Baptist church tradition, for instance, where infant baptism is not a custom, many congregations have a custom known as the "Cradle Roll." The Cradle Roll is a listing of all the infants in the congregation and their parents, supervised and kept up to date by a designated member who often is also designated to visit in the hospital and in the home. A member may, in fact, request a special service called "Dedication" in which the infant is dedicated to God. The mother, father, and infant are often the subject of prayers or announcements in the church bulletin. Thus, in all traditions, the arrival of a new life is an occasion for celebration.

In traditions which do practice infant baptism, the baptismal ceremony becomes the focal point for this celebration of adding a new life to the congregation and to the world. Where godparents are selected, these individuals assume duties in relation to the child. Where congregational forms of government and belief prevail, all the members of the congregation are the godparents, and the baptism service can only be held in the context of a regular congregational worship service, not separately with only family present. The child is viewed as having been born into a covenant community and the celebration of baptism seals the new person as a "child of the covenant" and as a member of the congregation itself.

The celebration aspect of baptism is an important one. It is in this celebration that the network of ties connecting this infant to the world is extended outward from the individual to a social fabric of concerned coparticipants in a human community. In a world in which we search for supportive structures for our common life, and in which human cooperation often breaks down in the face of conflicting interests and goals, these occasions of celebration become pivotal in the perpetuation of the life of the species.

Ceremonies, Celebrations and Community

One of the singular possessions of our species in comparison to all other animal life is the ability to arrange meaningless sounds and behaviors into elaborate symbol systems and to enact these over and over through rituals and ceremonial times. Throughout the history of the evolution of humanity, these ritual celebrations of cultural meanings and beliefs have served as a kind of social glue to weld together diverse elements of a group. The human community is a rich and beautiful kaleidoscope of life cycles and seasonal changes translated into rites and rituals, enacted with strictest form, and containing the most intricate set of rules for structural regularity. As bearers of a particular culture, we carry these rules around in our heads and put them to work when the occasion arises. We become teachers of our faith when we act out the rules together with others—infants, children, young, and old—in the ceremonies surrounding our common life as humans. At the same time, while we are teaching and learning, we are sharing in the creation of webs of people and of meanings that hold together the faith community of which we are a part.

Baptism is one of these socially crucial ceremonies. It cannot be understood alone or out of its context. It fits into the unfolding process of rites of passage that interlock throughout the life cycle, in which individuals are successively incorporated and initiated into, and ushered out of, each successive stage of human social experience. It takes its place in the succession of celebrations that mark the ongoing of individual lives within culture and within the context of the believing, celebrating, scattered-and-gathered fabric of life that we know as the human community.

· 4 ·

Anthropology
and Liturgy

The study of folk liturgy as ritual in preindustrial societies is one of the oldest and most important interests in cultural anthropology. Anthropologists using the methods of ethnography (descriptive work based on firsthand observation) have for a half century produced ritual studies on the meaning of symbols, the structure of activity, the use of space, the sacred objects, the leaders and participants, and on how symbolic enactments relate to the ongoing life of a society. Few, however, have attempted to study the ceremonial life of Anglo-Saxon Protestantism using these methods and models. This chapter explores the question of why Protestant anthropologists have avoided their own religion and culture in the analysis of liturgical forms and how such a study adds to our understanding of ritual life and to the creative design of programs for change.

The Dilemma of Marginality

Anthropologists who work in their own society are constantly balanced on a tightrope. They risk the constant danger of either falling into the chasm of subjectivity that is feared by all scientists or of becoming caught immobilized by the conflicts of attempting to be objective about their own cultural meanings, values, and beliefs. This conflict is especially real to those who study belief systems, religion, communal life, or the structure and process of liturgy within formal religion or folk culture. The culture under scrutiny is one's own, and the drive for objectivity may lead to the loss of cherished treasures of myth, symbols, and sustaining beliefs. The position of the ethnographer-anthropologist in this situation is one of cultural marginality.

For the past ten years I have been studying my own people, the white Anglo-Saxon Protestants of the American South, and in the process have become interested in the phenomenon of cultural marginality. I am interested in this phenomenon in part because of my own experience of taking on a role I have come to call that of a "marginal communicant" and then of becoming reabsorbed into the faith community from which I sprang. Cultural marginality also interests me because it is my suspicion that many would-be ethnographers of modern Christianity are frightened away from documenting the liturgies of morning worship, family night supper, and prayer meeting because of their conflicts about being marginal in their own society. Every person wants to be a part of a reference group, a group of individuals who provide self-definition and social support. Academic social scientists are no less human. They find this supportive group most frequently among a community of other intellectuals who may have temporarily or permanently dropped away from their own religious cultures or origin. Support may also be found from individuals who segment their lives into the daily routines of academic professionalism and the weekly routines of Sunday morning attendance at church as a way of compartmentalizing their intellectual, analytical activities from those more subjective and emotional ones related to their religious beliefs.

The process through which anthropologists have traditionally separated themselves from their religious backgrounds and formed their own new religion with its own myths, symbols, and liturgies is an interesting one. This process is undergone to some degree by other social scientists and by academics in general; it is more true of anthropologists, however, because of the crucial role of the fieldwork experience in shaping the new professional. Even though only a few have attempted the study of their own religious sub-culture, there is great potential for anthropological work using ethnography and cultural analysis in the study of churches and religious groups. This type of study can be invaluable in deepening the understanding of church people and seminary students and in contributing to the overall enrichment of Christian education. First, I will look at the way anthropologists are trained for the study of culture, then at the example of my own research on Protestant folk liturgy. Finally, I will discuss the uses of this kind of knowledge in the education of ministers and in consulting with churches and denominational agencies.

The Discipline of Anthropology

Anthropology has traditionally been defined as "the study of man"; it is now being redefined as "the study of the human species and of culture." Within this broad definition many kinds of inquiry take place. One is the analysis of species development through biological anthropology; another, the analysis of prehistoric cultures in the practice of archaeology. Other anthropologists study the structure of human language through linguistics, and the structure of human society and culture through social and cultural anthropology. These last two modes of doing anthropology—social and cultural—are those in which I work, using the methods of the ethnographer to collect data and the analytical tools of the cultural theorists and the theorists of society to place my data within manageable, understandable frameworks.

Within this big picture of the species as a social and cultural entity, I operate with certain sets of assumptions that come both from natural history and from culture theory. These assumptions include the understanding of humans as biosocial creatures who live out their biogram —the natural cycles from birth to death—within communities. Human communities are more than animal communities because of the possession of culture, the patterned set of rules for behavior that humans learn as a part of society.[1] It is the dimension of culture that separates us from other species and gives us our humanness. Each culture is specific and has its own patterned set of regularities, and at the same time all human culture operates according to certain overarching regularities that can be discerned and described. Describing and attempting to understand one individual cultural system is the task of ethnography; the ethnographer is the researcher who lives among a people for long periods of time in order to understand and describe their way of life. Placing this information in the larger context and comparing it to information on other cultures that are similar and different is the task of the science of ethnology. Ethnographers are also ethnologists when they attempt to explain cultural phenomena by resorting to theoretical explanations.

Part of the training of the ethnographer-ethnologist is the subjection of the person during graduate study to a rigorous reprogramming through which the customs, habits, beliefs, etc., of the scholarly and scientific community are substituted for those of an individual's own cultural community of orientation. Part of becoming an anthropologist, or of becoming a social scientist of any discipline, is the relinquishing of symbols and myths that are a part of older belief systems and the replacement of these with the symbols and myths congruent with the new belief system of the society known as *academia*, the university community. It is this process of reprogramming that creates ethnographers who are able to look objectively at the practices and beliefs of cultures around the world and then to make scientific comparisons between cultures without taking value positions. This reprogramming is a useful and needed mechanism for the socialization of professional ethnographers and ethnologists. It parallels the socialization process by which undergraduates are turned into doctors, who belong to the medical cultural system, or into lawyers, who belong to the subculture of jurisprudence. These types of learning experiences are also parallel to the enculturation of a child into the community of birth, the culture of origin. It is through the adoption of the rules of behavior and the symbols of articulate expression of cultural regularities that any person takes on his or her cultural identity.

Anthropologists as Marginal Communicants

Cultural marginality is a condition in which the individual who has been taught new values and rules is placed in a position on the edge of two cultures—the old and the new. Anthropologists have described the marginal position in preindustrial cultures of those individual native people who have been exposed to "the outside world." Frequently the native persons who have been to a mission school or have served as interpreters for traders, missionaries, or other outsiders are the persons most likely to adopt the anthropologist as their own personal project. Marginal people do not fit neatly into the central social and cultural matrix anymore once they have been away or have been to school, so they frequently become the natural contacts for the anthropologist, who is a representative of the outside world.

Morris Frieleich has described the condition of the anthropologist in the field as that of a "marginal native" because after a year or more the visiting researcher has certainly learned the cultural rules of the group under study; yet that person can never become a true native, no matter how great the desire to belong.[2] By the same token, when anthropologists return to their own culture, the experience of having been away into "the outside world" has opened new vistas and has changed their perception of the culture of their own childhood and even of the culture of academia into which they were so carefully socialized. Individuals in between two worlds are marginal individuals. Extending this model to apply to those who come out of the culture of modern Christianity, move into another culture, and then move back, I have called these people "marginal communicants." They have new eyes and new insights and can analyze the culture of their origin with new acuity if only they are stouthearted enough to attempt this difficult balance of objectivity and love.

Marginal communicants are often perched precariously on the edge of a congregation and of a denominational way of life. The people on the edges are all those who have been away into a far country, either adacemic or ideological, and have returned with hesitancy to a household where they were uncertain of whether they would be received. The academic prodigals are among the ones who became infatuated with the beliefs of scientism, of nihilism, of pure humanism, or of any belief system and set of cultural behavioral rules advocating other ways of life than the one into which they were socialized as children. Some embraced these new systems of thought and of action and have remained outside the community of their orientation. Others have shifted communities because of creative shifts in their own commitment or in their personal theologies. Still others participate intermittently in rituals and ceremonies of their religious community while living their day-to-day routines quite outside of these contexts. The particular problems associated with cultural marginality to one's own religious community are, I am convinced, in part responsible for the absence of ethnographic work on cultural liturgy within Protestant and Roman Catholic Christianity.

Sociologists of religion and other social scientists who approach the study of contemporary religious life with questionnaires and survey instruments for ascertaining "religiosity" or "attitudes toward religion" are at somewhat of an advantage in maintaining their scientific objectivity while studying a community of which they might have once been a part, or in which they continue to participate selectively. The ethnographer, on the other hand, uses methods that require immersion in the life-ways of the people under study. The most venerable tool in the ethnographic toolkit is the technique of participant observation. It is through participant observation that most ethnographer-anthropologists gather their information—by living with a society, talking with the people, discovering the invisible and unspoken rules for behavior and social relationships.

Using the ethnographic method to study congregational life or religious communal groups requires that ethnographers lay aside their own personal prejudices (at least temporarily) and their own personal biases about appropriate religious behavior, worship forms, Christian education programs, and human interaction. Dyed-in-the-wool liberal ethnographers who are studying mixed congregations of many views must maintain political neutrality in order to understand fully the position of a conservative faction. Ethnographers who are trained or experienced in early childhood education must refrain from telling the Sunday School superintendent how to organize or furnish a church nursery. Instead, they must observe and record sensitively the process through which the decisions are made on this problem. The person who believes in High Church liturgical forms and the drama of the Mass, must carefully avoid any condescending remark about the simplicity of a morning worship where there are few visible symbols and a minimum of formality. Instead, this service must be recorded in terms of its flow of action, its relation of people and events, its use of informal, non-traditional symbols to convey meanings that are at the heart of the nonhierarchical world view being expressed.

The ethnographer of congregational life or of religious communities must know enough about theology and modern religious thought to understand the nuances of the behavior, activities, and content of the action. The most important skill, however, is the skill of nonjudgmental observation and meticulous recording of detail in order to discover the exact ways that theologies and cultural values are translated into the actions that comprise human cultural communities. The ethnographer is not doing a study to prove or disprove one theology or to grind the axe for a point of view. The purpose of an ethnographic account is to uncover the subtle regularities of behavior and belief that are at the heart of culture and to detail the ways in which culture is expressed in each separate form of community in American denominationalism.

When I have explained this calculated distance approach to groups of seminary students or to students interested in change, those wishing to make things better than they are, I have often been asked how it is possible for me as a human being to maintain objectivity in the face of my own values and my own agendas for change. It is a difficult position, that of cultural marginality; and yet it is the only position that will enable any ethnographic worker to successfully detail the delicate grooves of culture and to bring them into light for deeper understanding. I believe it is essential, before we attempt to change people or congregations or the world, that we first be able to understand realistically and thoroughly all the kinds of forces that interplay within our cultural-community habitat. Through an understanding of the congregation as a small society, of the church as a segment of American culture and social organization, of the historical processes that have brought us to where we are, and of the cultural structures and patterns that make up the formal rules we live by, we may be able to design plans for change that have a higher degree of success— or we might decide that certain aspects of the system should be left alone and not changed at all. Ethnographers who are marginal communicants are faced with the imperative to be objective enough to view their own culture analytically and to be compassionate enough to wish for it to be better.

It is with this imperative, operating within the constraints of my disciplinary background of anthropology, that I set out in 1970 to study the Southern Presbyterians, a study that has now led me beyond this group of my own origins into studies of other Southern denominations and of Scottish culture and community. It is the imperative for both analysis and change which impels the marginal communicants to continue investigating the culture of American denominational life in congregations and in religious-familial expressions and to seek to understand this culture in comparative perspective with European and non-European societies.

The Anthropologist at Work

My first ethnographic study was carried out in the summer of 1970 as a participant observer, ethnographer, and marginal communicant in the summer community of Montreat, North Carolina, where members of the Presbyterian Church in the United States (the Southern Presbyterians) hold conferences and family gatherings. In late May I arrived in Black Mountain, North Carolina by bus, carrying my suitcase and typewriter, and began a three-month experience that was to prefigure my research for the next eight years. It was at Montreat that I learned to appreciate the patterned symbolic enactment of a culture that I now call "folk liturgy."

The people of Montreat begin to assemble for their summer-long ceremony in early June, when the 418 houses begin to fill with mothers and children coming to spend weeks or months reestablishing ties with family and kin and with old friends. Their summer life is the life of the separated rural retreat congruent with their classical Celtic church history as Presbyterians. Fathers appear and disappear in week-end rhythms; grandparents are brought in from the towns and cities and from the nursing homes to enjoy the aura of family attention and the honors of age. Children as young as four and five years toddle off with big brothers and sisters in the morning to attend young peoples' clubs, and teen-agers and college students circle in and out as they perform tasks of cleaning, food-service, building-maintenance, supervision of the children, or as they meet and begin romances with others in their age group. The separateness of Montreat from the everyday routines of city and town life, the separation of the kinship networks from their winter associations in the assimilated world of the city, and the bounding of Presbyterians from non-Presbyterians operate to establish Montreat as a classical sacred community, a type of monastery that includes all the family of faith instead of only the celibate monks of the early monastic communities.

The liturgy that accompanies the celebration of this summer-long worship experience is one based on family loyalty and religious allegiance, a liturgy growing from and feeding into the value system described earlier as religious familism. The patterned gatherings for the community of cottage people include the front-porch kin visit, the family gathering or family reunion, the cottage-owners' picnic (which for our visiting anthropologist from Mars would be difficult to separate from the family reunion in its action sequences, process of activities, and its use of sacred symbols), the Fourth of July, the Club Leaders' Talent Show, and the weekly 11:00 A.M. worship in the auditorium (which is the ritual high point of the week and where the entire community assembles to greet one another in fluid clusters along the wide lawn outside the door after the service.) The sacred symbols that appear and reappear in these events include the family cottage itself, handed down from generation to generation; the pictures and genealogies that form the focus for many a long session of storytelling by grandmother and the aunts while sitting on the porch or by the fire; and the food items that are brought to the family gathering or to a communal meal among families who are friends. Certain food items are especially associated with these ceremonial occasions: fried chicken, potato salad, and other items for the family reunion; waffles or pancakes, locally picked blackberries from the mountain, or fruit and vegetables from the fresh foods market near the Montreat gate for the joint meal among families.

The Montreat community provides a format for the repeated restatement of cultural symbols and the repeated reestablishment of kinship and friendship ties among a scattered people. In the participation over many summers of the unfolding strata of ages and of family cycles, an individual learns to become an adult in the culture appropriate to a proper Presbyterian way of life. My life as an anthropologist with the Montreat community gave me a new appreciation for the tenacity of cultural tradition in the face of urbanization and population movements. It also gave me an awareness of the intricately patterned segments that form cultural liturgies and the importance of these liturgies in even the most modern industrial society.

My second foray into the cultural world of American religious groups was really a whole series of ethnographic studies. In an attempt to identify and delineate the various types of gatherings in addition to the summer religious communities that provide loci for symbolic expression of culture in the American South, I became a marginal member of numerous day-long or week-long liturgies expressing intertwined religious and familial themes. At family reunions in the country I ate fried chicken and drank iced tea and visited through long summer Sunday afternoons with elderly ladies who served as "family historians" and with young mothers holding their babies on their laps. I listened to homecoming sermons and had dinner-on-the-grounds at rural churches in open-country neighborhoods. In August I sat under wooden arbors with sawdust floors to hear campmeeting preachers extol the virtues of repentance and the godly life. All three of these types of gatherings contained elements of the cultural pattern of religious familism that is associated with the southern United States. All exhibit some of the same features seen at Montreat—family loyalty based on descent from a common ancestor, attachment to a rural retreat from the world of the city, and religious practices centered in traditional patterns of worship and traditional denominational ties. These repetitive ceremonial assemblages are a vehicle for continuing and transmitting culture among people who are otherwise widely scattered urban dwellers and who, without the assemblies, would have no opportunity to continue their network and to express their culture beyond the individual family or congregation.

The search for comparative data on similar types of recurrent rituals led me into my third fieldwork project, three summers of ethnographic work among the people of the Scottish regions of the ancestry of many Protestant Southerners. The clan gatherings of the Scottish Highlands, the church anniversaries and jubilees in the Southwest, and the town festivals of the Borders are gatherings that serve to assemble widely scattered people for kin-religious events. Like the scattered town and urban dwellers of the American South, the residents of Edinburgh, Glasgow, and numerous English cities return to their places of origin and restore family ties periodically in ceremonies giving symbolic expression to deeply rooted cultural themes.

The pitfalls of marginality are not so great when I am living in a Scottish community or when I am delineating the liturgical form of the gathering of the clan. These people are "my people" only in the anthropological sense, not in the sense of original socialization and values. The liturgies of the culture I am observing can be seen in an objective way, relatively free of ethnocentric biases. As an ethnographer in Scotland I am a representative of the outside in the truest sense. I live on the edge of the town on a working sheep farm. I attend and record the local church anniversaries, the town's festival day, the children's picnic, the church's morning worship, and the women's group coffee mornings. I go to the North for a clan gathering and to the Southwest to visit a noted rural church. I sit in front of my cottage on a sunny afternoon and answer the questions of the farmer's seven-year-old daughter, who wants to know about oceans, airplanes, and Atlanta, Georgia. I am an outsider and, therefore, because they are not my own, the liturgies of daily life and the highly stylized liturgy of the ceremonies I record in my notebook are more comfortable to study.

Beyond Marginality—The Uses of Anthropology for Education and Change

My discussion of cultural marginality has treated the process through which anthropologists in the ethnographic tradition are turned into marginal communicants in their own culture in order to be able to study other societies objectively. As an example of the ethnographic study of religious groups and of the process of doing anthropological fieldwork, I have referred to my own journey through several related research projects in which I gradually became aware of the benefits and the difficulties associated with this type of study. I am convinced at this point that the benefits and promises of ethnographic study and its potential application to solving educational and change problems far outweigh the disadvantages of cultural marginality. In conclusion, I will mention several of these possible applied areas—those of classroom teaching, analysis of community and culture for deepened understanding, and the use of anthropological knowledge for problem solving.

The first and most traditional application is in the classroom situation of teaching and learning. While the college or university classroom is not that of a church, it contains church members and nonchurch individuals who will eventually shape the society of the next few decades. The appreciation of culture as a system, and its infinite variability worldwide, opens a window of understanding for students who may be making decisions on foreign policy or educational programs within the not-too-distant future. It is important for them to analyze and appreciate their own culture as well as other cultures as they shape their values and goals and develop intellectual acuity.

Cultural and social anthropology taught to future ministers in seminary classrooms becomes an even closer application of this knowledge to Christian education. Just as all people from the outside are marginal to a group, ministers are marginal to congregations in certain ways. They bring into each pastorate their ideas and beliefs about how churches ought to operate, how educational programs ought to be organized, and how people ought to believe. They seldom have an awareness that they are representatives from the outside world of the seminary and the denominational hierarchical tradition in a small cultural system already embedded in the congregational community. Through understanding the cultural grooves of the many "little traditions" of American denominational life in every region, ministers may develop a sense of awe—as I did at Montreat—at the delicate nature of cultural organization and social structures intertwined with beliefs and values. They may be better able not only to change their congregations with these understandings, but they may also be better able to accept them as they are.

Away from the classroom setting the uses and applications of anthropological knowledge can already be found in numerous areas of American life—including those of education in cross-cultural settings, the building of urban renewal houses that people will live in, and the designing of hospitals and medical delivery services that are congruent with the culture of the people to be served. This same type of applied anthropology is appropriate, I believe, in the design of churches that meet space needs within cultural prescriptions, of educational programs that are conceived and structured with the culture of the recipients in mind, and of congregational liturgies at both folk and formal levels that are congruent with cultural practices. This type of designing does not mean a dilution of theological teachings or of doctrinal prescriptions for education or worship. What it does mean is a sensitivity to the facts of our humanness and to the delicacy of the existing patterns of social and cultural arrangements. It means that one program designed and packaged in the central denominational office in Philadelphia or Atlanta will not fit every congregation. It means that Christians who are Episcopalian, Presbyterian, Methodist, or members of other denominations are also Europeans, Southerners, White, Black, Asian, Chicano, or of other culturally defined categories which have their own traditions and behaviors. It means understanding that human groups are slow to change and that folk liturgies and cultural traditions are valuable aspects of ongoing life that should be treasured and not trounced upon.

It is the uses of anthropological knowledge in implementing programs of change that church people are eager to know about. "How can we change these people who do not want to adopt new curriculum, new forms of worship, or new confessional statements?" they ask. It is a difficult question—that of how anthropological knowledge, or knowledge of any social science, can assist in problem solving when conflicts arise over these deeply rooted convictions. The answer must be an ambivalent one. It cannot always help, but it may provide insights that can then assist both sides in the change situation.

In the 1940s the Department of Agriculture of the United States Government hired anthropologists to analyze the social organization of traditional farms in order to understand ways to implement change programs. During the same period the Bureau of Indian Affairs employed anthropologists to describe and interpret the social organization and culture tradition of various native American peoples on reservations so that the programs of the BIA could be better designed and local cultures would not be destroyed in the process of modernization. At the present time, applied anthropologists work in schools, hospitals, public health care programs, and urban housing as consultants and advisers whose knowledge of social structure and culture can be used to bring about changes that are constructive, so that problems of value conflict and belief conflict can be resolved with sensitivity to both or all views. It is this kind of outside-insider advising that might be valuable to church congregations, to denominational boards and agencies, and to the planners of social action at the district or presbytery level. By making wise use of the role of marginal communicant, the anthropologist might provide invaluable advice and planning assistance in bringing about constructive change.

The role of marginal communicant is difficult, and for this reason few anthropologists will decide to accept it.

Walking on a tightrope is never a comfortable activity. But for those who risk studying their own culture of origin—Protestant, Roman Catholic, Jewish, or other—and who are willing to stand in the relation of nonintrusive advisers, or of sympathetic assistants in change, the rewards will be lodged in the enrichment of their own knowledge and understanding and in the benefits that result for the church and the society.

PART II

The Christian Life in Liturgical Context

John H. Westerhoff, III

· 5 ·

Liturgy and Catechesis:
A Christian Marriage

Professor Neville has expanded our understanding of
the function of ritual as a necessary aspect of our
common life. As an anthropologist, she has significantly
increased our knowledge of liturgy and learning by bringing scholarly objectivity to her investigation of religion
and religious life in our day. Now we turn to learning
within the Christian community of faith and the admittedly confessional attempt of a professor-priest to bring
scholarly subjectivity to an exploration of learning
within the church.

Liturgy and learning have been linked since the birth
of the Christian era, but of late they have become estranged. Regretfully, religious educators and liturgists
have gone their separate ways and attempts to reunite
their various concerns have tended to confuse the issue
and distort important distinctions between them. Some
religious educators have made the serious mistake of
speaking of teaching *by* or *with* the liturgy, thereby re-
ducing the liturgy to a didactic act. To *use* the liturgy is
to do it violence. Of course, we learn through the liturgy,
hence the title of this book. Our rituals shape and form
us in fundamental ways. But our liturgies should be
understood properly as ends and not as means.

Nevertheless, both liturgy and catechesis are pastoral
activities through which divine revelation is made
known, mature faith is enhanced and enlivened, and per-

sons are prepared and stimulated for their vocation in the world. Perhaps the best way to differentiate between them is this: Liturgy is the actions and catechesis the reflections of the community of faith. Together they form the praxis (reflective action) by which the community is made aware of who and whose it is; learns that for which and by which it is called to live and die; and comes to understand why life is as it is, as well as, more importantly what it is to become. Liturgy nurtures the community of faith through celebrative symbolic acts of faith. Catechesis nurtures the community of faith through mindful attempts to communicate and reflect upon the story (myth) which underlies and informs these acts of faith. One is not the other. But the life of faith and the community of faith cannot exist without both. And faithful life implies their integration.

The Church is the family of God, a visible, historical, human community called to nurture its people in the Gospel tradition so that they might live under the judgment and inspiration of the Gospel to the end that God's will is done and God's community comes. The church is the body of Christ, a hidden, prophetic creature of God's spirit, an instrument of God's transforming power and a witness to God's continuing revelation in history.

It is one church, a paradox to the mind; sinful yet holy; divided, yet one; continuously in need of reform, yet the bearer of God's converting Word: a human institution, but also a holy community; a disparate assembly of baptized sinners living, sometimes unconsciously, by grace, but also an intentional, obedient, steadfast, faithful company of converted visible saints; a mystery even to itself, but aware, in often incomprehensible ways, that it has a mission in the world and a ministry to those who by birth or decision find themselves, not entirely by choice within that family which bears the name Christian.

This church of Jesus Christ, God's people, has a mission in the world and on behalf of the world. And this church, God's people, has a ministry to those who have been called, named, and commissioned to live in and for God's coming community so that they might be prepared, equipped, and stimulated for faithful life in God's service. In order for this company of Gospel bearers to faithfully witness through word and deed, the church will need to reform its life of liturgy and catechesis.

Catechesis

Catechesis is essentially a pastoral activity intended to enable the people of God to meet the twofold responsibility which Christian faith requires of them: community with God and neighbor. It is the process by which persons come to know (understand), internalize (live), and apply (do) God's Word in their individual and corporate lives. Catechesis values the interaction of "faithing" souls in community, striving to be faithful in-but-not-of the world. As such, catechesis aids us to understand the implications of the Christian tradition for our life and lives, to critically evaluate every aspect of our individual and corporate understandings and ways, and to become equipped and inspired for faithful action in church and society.

Catechesis includes knowing, loving, and obeying God's Word; social service and action is the church addressing the individual and corporate needs of those denied the benefits of God's intentions; evangelism is the church witnessing in word and deed its faith in God's good news; stewardship is the church expressing God's will for individual and corporate life in the world; pastoral care is the church ministering to the material and spiritual needs of all people; fellowship (church life) is the church providing a sign of God's kingdom; administration is the church ordering and organizing its common life of mission and ministry; worship is the church providing a context for confrontation with, commitment to, and empowerment by the "Word of God".

Catechesis is the means by which the community becomes aware of God's revelation, comes to faith, and acquires mature knowledge, understanding, and commitment so as to judge and evaluate its life of social action, evangelism, stewardship, pastoral care, administration, worship, and fellowship. It prepares and stimulates persons and the community for faithful mission and ministry through every aspect of its corporate life.

Catechesis is the means by which the church seeks to understand faith's requirements for its liturgical life, to evaluate and reform its liturgies from the perspective of this faith, and to prepare the community for faithful participation in its liturgies.

"By their rites you will know them" is more than mere rhetoric. We humans cannot live without ritual or exist without shared understandings of the world and established correct ways of living. These understandings and ways (faith) are expressed collectively through symbolic narratives (sacred stories) and symbolic acts (rites and rituals). Through its "rites of community" (following the calendar, once a week or year), the church sustains and transmits its faith. Through "rites of initiation and life crises" the church enables persons to make transitions in their faith pilgrimage and life cycle.

Perhaps no aspect of community life is more important than its rites and rituals. We humans are made for ritual and, in turn, our rituals make us. No culture is complete without common beliefs and ceremonial practices. A community's understandings and ways are invariably objectified in ceremonial observances. No people have ever been discovered who fail to share some articulated set of beliefs about the world and their place in it, expressed in community myths. And nowhere is there a people who fail to engage in symbolic acts to sustain and transmit their myths. Faith and ritual cannot be separated. That explains why, when the prophets sensed that the people had forsaken their faith, they attacked their rituals, but when the people had lost their faith they called them to return to their rituals.

Worship is at the center of the church's life. Orthodoxy implies right ritual. The rites and rituals of a Christian faith community are central to the church's life. Perhaps that is why our rituals are so difficult to change. We all know that it is easier and more acceptable to preach a radical sermon than it is to change the order of worship. The structures of our rituals provide us with a means for ordering and reordering our lives. Our rituals telescope our understandings and ways, unite us in community, give meaning and purpose to our lives and provide us with purposes, guides, and goals for living. That explains why, when our understandings and ways of life change, we will very likely cease to participate in the rituals that once inspired and sustained us. It is also why, after casting aside old rituals, we seek to birth new ones.

Changes in our understandings and ways result in changes in our ritual life. And changes in our rituals produce significant changes in our understandings and ways. That is why some people want the church's rituals to change and others do not. Most every reform movement in the history of the church has involved liturgical change. Indeed the most revolutionary changes in Christian history have resulted from liturgical reform. Reformations and ritual renewal go hand in hand.

Karl Marx rightly observed that religion can either be

an opiate of the masses or a prophetic protest against injustice and in support of change. Whether it will be an opiate or a prophetic protest will be influenced by the shape and content of our rituals.

Without the support of meaningful rituals (symbolic actions), there is no meaningful personal life or political social action. Liturgy, the activity of the community, unites symbolic and social actions. Each needs and supports the other. To deny either one is to deny the whole. Liturgy, the life of the community, includes discipleship within the community expressed through ritual and apostleship in the world by personal and social actions. Insofar as we have neglected our rituals, we have starved and discouraged apostleship in the world. Because we have failed to understand the important unity between our rituals and lives, we have both improperly prepared persons for meaningful participation in the faith community's ceremonial life and continued to encourage persons to participate mindlessly in rituals which often are antithetical to Christian faith. Only when we grasp the centrality of ritual for the church's life will the educational mission of the Christian church be realizable.

The Nature of the Christian Faith

At the heart of the Christian faith is a story. Indeed, at the heart of every community's life is a story—a story that explains its understanding of the world, the place of persons in that world, and the ways of life they are to pursue. One essential role of ritual is to communicate the community's story in ways that help it become internalized and acted upon. Catechesis also shares a concern for making the community's story *our* story. Too often, however, very different stories are being communicated and learned in the church. The educator's responsibility is to help the community get its story straight.

The Christian story is a story of God's mighty deeds, God's actions in history. It is a story about a vision. In the beginning God had a vision of a world at one with itself, a world of peace, justice, freedom, equity, whole community, and the well-being of all. This is the world God intends.

God creates persons in "his" (her) image as historic actors whom God intends to live in and for God's vision. But God also grants us the freedom to say yes or no to this vision. And so the plot thickens. We humans seem to be more interested in our visions than in God's vision. We create systems (principalities and powers) which benefit some of us but not all of us. As a result of our own selfish actions we become isolated from nature, ourselves, each other, and God.

But God persists in seeking after us. God calls a community, our foreparents, into being to witness to God's vision. And God takes the side of those who are either kept outside or oppressed by the systems we humans create. God, biased to the hurt and the have-nots, acts on their behalf that "her" vision might be realized. God liberated our foreparents in Egypt, patiently pulled them toward "his" vision, and established a covenant with them to live as God's visionary community. Still it did not work. It seems that as soon as we humans begin to receive the blessings of God's vision we act to keep these blessings for ourselves alone. But God continues to raise up prophets to remind us of God's intentions for the world, and a faithful remnant keeps the story of God's vision alive.

Nevertheless, it is as if we are in bondage to the social forces, to political, economic, and social systems we humans have built. Over and over again some individuals catch a glimpse of God's vision and commit their lives to its realization. Yet that vision still remains a lost dream. So God makes a decision. God acts again, enters our human condition, becomes incarnate in Jesus of Nazareth, the storyteller, dreamer, doer of deeds, healer of hurts, advocate of the outsider, liberator of the oppressed. Through Jesus the good news is announced: God's community has come. In the absurdity and foolishness of the cross God acts to liberate us from bondage to the principalities and powers. Nothing—no social, political, or economic power—can hold us any longer. And so on Easter morning the disciples behold the dawn of God's coming community.

Yet the dawn of hope is not yet the high noon of God's community come on earth. Darkness still covers much of the land, people are still oppressed, wars continue, poverty and hunger prevails, injustice is perpetuated, and the mass of humanity is still marginal to God's promise. Many of us who claim the name Christian continue to frustrate God's vision and live as if we do not understand the implications of its message. We bless our individualism and competition. We say this is the best of all possible worlds, and we justify our way of life.

Once again, God calls prophets forth to remind us of "his" vision and the radical demands it places on our lives. The Gospel itself judges and inspires us. Here and there some live according to God's will and for God's coming community. And each week the community of faith gathers to retell its story, to celebrate its hope, to point to the signs of God's coming community, to announce that we are liberated from the principalities and powers, and to stimulate us to act with God for "her" vision.[1]

The church is the bearer of this story. And when this story becomes *our* story we will know what the name Christian means. Liturgy is concerned that the story be known and lived. Catechesis is concerned that the story be understood and applied. We had better agree on the story.

Liturgy: The Work of God's Visionary People

Our rituals can be dangerous. They can act to bless and sustain the way things are in the world. They can induct people into accepting society as it is. Indeed, that is what every culture asks of its religious institutions and expects of their rites and rituals. But the God of the Christian faith asks something quite different. God calls the church to be a community of cultural change. Our rituals are to aid us in critically judging the world, to provide us with visions of the world God intends and to motivate us to live in God's world as strangers and pilgrims. Our rituals in the Christian church are meant to induct us into a community which is willing to live and die for the transformation of the world. The Christian faith is truly radical. It demands that we seek justice for all who are marginal, become advocates of the have-nots, liberate the oppressed, and seek the well-being of all.

Too often our ritual life provides an escape from the world and a support for the status quo. Too often our educational programs socialize us to uncritically accept and participate in such rituals. Liturgy—the work of God's visionary people—properly unites ritual (symbolic actions) and prophetic action. Our rituals must, if they are to be Christian, equip and motivate persons and the community to act in the world for social change. Likewise our prophetic actions must be informed and inspired by Christian understandings and ways communicated and sustained through meaningful rituals.

Our bodily actions influence our emotions and ways of thinking. We kiss our children not only because we love them but also in order to love them. Rituals are symbolic actions. Those which emphasize penitence may cause us to believe we are inadequate to addressing social issues; those expressive of transcendence as a separation of secular and sacred may cause us to withdraw from the world's problems; kneeling expressive of a return to the womb may encourage the privatization of life. On the other hand, standing may create a sense of corporate selfhood and community consciousness; rituals expressive of a redeemed community may influence a good feeling about ourselves and our potential; and those expressive of transcendence as a sacred-secular beyond may move us to involvement in the world.

Neither the pietist, who has no commitment to the struggle for justice and righteousness in the world of institutional life, nor the social activist, who has no personal commitment to Christ, is mature in Christian faith. Authentic Christian life is personal and social life lived on behalf of God's will in the political, social, and economic world. Piety (religious experience) and politics (prophetic action) belong together. Parish life (catechesis and liturgy) needs to support both and contribute to their union.

The Christian life is existence over against the status quo, existence committed to a vision of God's coming community of liberation, justice, peace, wholeness, and the well-being of all people. We cannot be nurtured into such a life—not in this world. Every culture strives to socialize persons to live in harmony with life as it is. But God calls "his" people to be signs of *shalom*, the vanguard of God's coming community, a community of cultural change as well as cultural continuity. To reach the conviction that such countercultural life is our Christian vocation, and to be enabled to live such a corporate existence in-but-not-of the world, necessitates reformed rituals and new corresponding forms of catechesis.

The church is best understood as a creation of God, a community of corporate social agents called to bear witness, individually and corporately, in word and deed, to God's intentions for human life. The church is called to be a radical community for others, a countercultural community biased to and acting with God on behalf of the oppressed, hurt, poor, and have-nots of the world. The church can never exist for itself. It is never an end, only a means. Its mission, its end, is to be a community where Christian faith is proclaimed, experienced, understood, lived, and acted upon. The unification of liturgy and catechesis is essential if the church is to be the community of faith God intends. Too often we have led persons through our liturgies to lives of mere inwardness or personal piety, thus blessing the existing social, political, and economic orders regardless of the injustices they may perpetuate. The covenant of God's people with the Lord of history entails responsibility for the total character of society. To restrict religion to the immediate relation between an individual and God, or to an individual's relationship with another individual, is pietism. Pietism is a turning from the God of the Christian faith, a denial of the sovereignty of God over the whole of life, and thus a heresy. To neglect the social world and institutional life is to deny the sovereignty of God over the whole of life; it is to practice an idolatry, for it confines God to individual existence and limits Christian life to individual behavior, thereby leaving the world to the principalities and powers.

God intends that the church be a witnessing community of faith, a converted pilgrim people living under the judgment and inspiration of the Gospel to the end that God's will is done and God's community comes. Unless our rituals support and encourage such radical existence, they are dubiously Christian. The educational ministry of the church needs to provide a way for the community to examine, judge, and reform its rituals in the light of this faith. And then, also, to provide the means for persons to prepare for meaningful participation in the community's rituals. To ignore this responsibility is to be ignorant of the central role ritual plays in the lives of people and their communities. A faithful strategy for education and ministry in the church, therefore, needs to unite liturgy and catechesis.

Ritual (symbolic action) is an essential aspect of all life. Indeed, it is our orderly, predictable, repetitive, symbolic actions which give life shape and form, meaning and purpose. Without ritual we lack a means for building and establishing community, identity, and at-oneness in the world; we are without a means for making the changes in our lives meaningful and integrating; and we are devoid of our most significant means for sustaining and transmitting our understandings and ways. Indeed, there is no cultural choice between ritual and no ritual, but only what our rituals will be. Ritual is foundational to life. In those historic moments when the church had lost its soul, it had neglected its ritual. Correspondingly, every reform in the history of the church has been at its core a reformation of ritual. When our rituals change, our lives change, and when we change our understandings and ways, we change our rituals.

Today is marked by new life in the community of faith. The prophets, as of old, have confronted us with the inadequacy of our rituals. While experimentation and change are necessary in this transitory period, marked by a new consciousness of the Gospel's call for justice and community, we long to secure ourselves in a sanctioned and valued structure of orderly, repetitive actions symbolic of our faith. The days of improvisation and change need to end, for in our secular, alien world, a community of renewed, reformed faith needs to establish new structured rituals.

The chief problem for life in a pluralistic, secular, technological, urban world is attaining, owning, and maintaining one's identity as a person and follower of Jesus Christ. The claims for loyalty are legion, and the diverse communities which ask our allegiance are many. Only an identity-conscious, tradition-bearing community, rich in meaningful ritual, can help us to know and remember who we are. Life is fragmented and compartmentalized. We search for wholeness and at-one-ness in what is often an alienating world. Vital community rituals alone can prevent us from spiritual dislocation and lostness.

The church cannot live with rituals that divide the generations as if they had nothing in common. We cannot afford to accept the separation of children, youth, and adults for distinctive rituals. Community is the gift of shared rituals. The needs of various persons may differ, but we grow only when we share our differences in community. Peer group isolation prevents growth. When we permit our rites of community to address the needs of some particular age group alone, everyone suffers. The norm for the church's community rite is the Lord's Supper or Eucharist, which by its very nature is inclusive of all.

The current craze in which everyone is encouraged to create their own rituals for various age groups can be divisive. The function of community rites is to form unity, not division. Besides, each generation needs the insights, experiences, and contributions of the others if any are to grow. We need to conserve a memory and maintain a tradition, just as we need to nurture visions and the incarnation of futuristic expressions. Without both continuity and change, we cannot maintain security and identity in the present. If our community rituals have ignored the needs of any generation, or have been dominated by any particular generation, they need to be reformed and reshaped until all feel at home in them, and all are stretched to newness of faith and life. My point is simple: We do not need special rites of community for children or youth, but we do need a place within our regular community rituals that speaks to children, youth and adults.

Further, the church needs to acknowledge the paradoxical nature of its faith and provide for both daily individual prayer in community and Sunday Eucharistic community rituals, sometimes in the form of penitential rites (Advent and Lent) and sometimes as the celebrations of a redeemed community.

The mission of the church is the compelling risk to live our common longings for the Gospel of Jesus Christ so that the community of God may be realized. The ministry of the church encompasses ways of believing, being, and behaving which contribute to this mission. Within this ministry, shared by all baptized persons, liturgics and catechesis must be united so that the community of faith might authentically celebrate the Eucharist in community and live the Eucharist in the world.

A Liturgical Catechesis

One challenge confronting the church is to integrate education, worship, fellowship, and service. At the core of this unified understanding of ministry is worship. And at the center of worship is God's Word. What follows, however, is not a program, but images of the corporate life of children, youth, and adults in the church which speaks to this integration.

But first a few thoughts to ponder. The norm for Christian life is the celebration of the Eucharist, best understood as a joyful gathering of God's storytelling people to proclaim their faith and share a common meal with their risen Lord so as to be united in community, refreshed and empowered for ministry in the world.

This festive gathering is not so much a private, passive, individualistic occasion as it is a public, active, corporate activity. It is not a subjective act in which we do something either for or to ourselves. Neither is it an objective act through which we do something either for or to God. Rather, it is an occasion for the community to gratefully encounter God in Jesus Christ and act *with* God in the transformation of life and of our lives.

In the most recent past we have tended to think of this Holy Communion in terms of our extreme unworthiness, depravity, and sin, a memorial for a dead friend or a solemn wake to mourn our condition. Is it not also necessary to understand Holy Communion in terms of our having been made worthy by Christ's passion and resurrection to stand joyfully before God—a cheerful thanksgiving, a victory party to celebrate God's good news?

Imagine a congregation in which such a festive Eucharist is at the heart of its common life. Within such a congregation children, youth, and adults can, along with their priest (the symbol bearer and presider who enables the people to act while keeping things in good order), might gather regularly to reflect upon and plan for its weekly celebration.

Imagine a congregation gathering for an hour of catechesis before the morning family Eucharist followed by a family fellowship meal at which reports and intentions for ministry in the world could be made and celebrated. At the heart of every Eucharist are the propers, the lessons, the assigned Scripture. During the week various youth and adults might gather with their priest to engage in serious Bible study and prepare for their worship. At this time they could appropriately decorate the place of worship; plan the hymns; prepare the prayers of the people; and plan for the sermon as a homily, dialogue, song, story, drama, or dance. They could bake the bread and make the wine to be offered. Further they might plan for an educational experience for all ages before the service to help them prepare to participate in the community liturgy.

In the context of a coffee-fellowship hour, in which new persons could be welcomed and the needs of people ministered to, the people could rehearse their celebration and explore together the week's Lessons. For example, the Noah story could be dramatized; persons could choose their favorite animal and paint it on a stole to be worn in the procession. Persons could then go about making their animal sounds until they found a mate to join them in the sung processional. Special days could be celebrated. For example, on June 29, the festival of Sts. Peter and Paul, the church could sponsor a Saturday fishing trip and letter-writing to the church on mission. Following the Eucharist could be a fish fry at which the letters are shared. Thus the unity of catechesis and liturgy in a missionary fellowship could evolve.[2]

Only our imaginations hinder the development of creative, corporate life in a learning and witnessing community of Christian faith. The challenge we face is clear: to integrate our lives of ministry and mission within a spirit-filled body of committed, baptized Christians who weekly gather to prepare and celebrate the Eucharist meaningfully, and scatter refreshed to live the Eucharist in the world. That is what it means to unite catechesis and liturgy within a faithful community of Christian faith.

·6·

Spiritual Life:
Ritual and Consciousness

The twentieth century is not likely to be known as the age of spirituality. More reasonably, it may be remembered as the era of retarded consciousness. Many have lost or forgotten the experience of God which lies at the heart of Christian faith. Still, we long and search for some sense of the divine: witness the renewed interest in the occult, Eastern religions, meditation, and personal religious experience. It is as if we humans knew we were more than rational beings and that truth was more than reason could prove. Even we moderns are *homo religiosus.* Prayer and ritual are still the most basic expressions of our humanness.

Aquinas wrote, "Prayer is the peculiar proof of religion." Faith, in Luther's judgment, was "prayer, nothing but prayer." Baron von Hugel concluded that "prayer is the essential element of all life." And Schleirmacher observed "to be religious and to pray are really the same thing." Still the word "prayer" lacks clarity. Some think of prayer as distressed cries to the heavens, others as a formality before meals and meetings, or an experience on mountain tops. Prayer for some is a spontaneous emotional discharge, and for others a fixed rational formula to be recited. However, prayer, as I am using the word, is a generic term to describe every aspect of our conscious relationship with God. Prayer represents what I mean by the spiritual life—daily existence lived in relationship with God—or piety, the daily activity of living in the presence of God through adoration, confession, praise, oblation, thanksgiving, and petition/intercession.

To live in adoration is to focus our life upon the heart and mind of God, asking nothing but to enjoy God's presence. It is the life of the lover, the dreamer and visionary, which makes possible viewing every aspect of life as a miracle. Confession is life lived under the judgment and grace of God. It is the life of those striving to bring their individual, interior experience and belief into harmony with their social exterior practice and action. The life of praise is a life alive with the memory of the mighty acts of God. It is a life of ecstasy, lived dancing, singing, and praising God even in evil days. Thanksgiving is our celebrative awareness of God's continuing actions in our historical midst. It is the life that can still spy burning bushes, hear the voice of God, and grasp the presence of Christ in contemporary culture. Oblation is an offering of ourselves, our lives and labors, for the purposes of God. Petition/intercession is the continuous striving to bring our wills in line with God's will. It is life lived in conscious loyalty to the conviction that Jesus is Lord, passing moral judgments on what is the means to be faithful.

The spiritual life, then, is an historical life lived with a conscious awareness of God's presence; it is life so lived that our minds, hearts, and wills are united with God's in common historical reflective action. Surely, this understanding rules out prayer in which the world or the self is depreciated or denied, in which the human personality is dissolved or absorbed into a unity with an otherworldly reality. Prayer is not a negative process moving us out of our normal state or condition, a passive, resigned contemplation of otherness, or a striving after emotional ecstasy through the extinction of thought or volition. Prayer is ultimately an ethical activity. History is the peculiar province of God's revelation and fellowship. Blessedness of life with God is life in this world; it is in our daily lives that we meet and have communion with God.

For such an understanding of prayer to prevail we need to recover the proper place of religious experience. The popularity of the charismatic and Jesus movements are evidence of our neglect of experience, but that does not mean that we ought to turn uncritically to speaking in tongues, pseudomysticism, exotic forms of meditation, or uncontrolled emotion. The switch from doctrine and dogma to either silence or glossalalia is no solution. Nor is the switch from formal institutional and ceremonial life to simplistic emotional commitment to Jesus. Spiritual euphoria without social action may be religious, but it is not Christian. Personal ecstasy is no substitute for social justice. "Thy kingdom come" is an essential petition of Jesus' prayer; *Maranatha*, "Come Lord Jesus," the central petition of the early church. Both call us to live in a conscious relationship to God's kingdom. Prayer or true religious experience, for the Christian, is living in communion with God in the midst of personal and social history making.

The Christian life focuses upon the spirit of God in us and in the world; its quest is for an active unity with the God of history. The climax of the Christian life is not enlightenment but unification with the will and activity of God. Christian prayer assumes both an historical awareness and the integration of the receptive and active modes of consciousness.

Numerous examples of prayer in the Bible support this understanding. The Scriptures assume an historicist perspective. Operating from that perspective, the prophets used their intuitive ability to hear the voice of God and their intellects to proclaim a judgment on the people for their lack of righteousness and on the nations for their lack of justice. Moses' experience with the burning bush led him to bring to his people a vision and message of liberation. Jesus' struggle at Gethsemane led him to make a conscious decision to choose the foolishness of the cross. The awareness of the presence of Christ in the breaking of bread at Emmaus led the disciples to lives of apostleship. Paul's experience on the road to Damascus led him to change from persecutor to defender of the faith. None of these experiences or their resulting actions were purely rational or intuitional. Each represents a worldly intuitive experience which, through the complementary use of the intellect, led to new sorts of moral behavior. Each represents finally a new worldly consciousness of God and praxis according to God's will. Each is an example of prayer.

Let me, therefore, suggest that catechesis for prayer requires first that we help persons to regain their God-given ability to wonder and create; to dream, fantasize, imagine, and envision; to sing, paint, dance, and act; their natural capacity for ecstasy, for appreciating the new, the marvelous, the mysterious, and for sensual and kinesthetic awareness; their God-given talent to express themselves emotionally, and nonverbally.

To demonstrate, let me share a Sufi story: Nasrudin sometimes took people for trips in his boat. One day a pedagogue hired him to ferry him across a very wide river. As soon as they were afloat, the scholar asked him whether it was going to be rough.

"Don't ask me nothing about it," said Nasrudin.

"Have you never studied grammar?"

"No," said the Mulla.

"In that case half your life has been wasted."

The Mulla said nothing. Soon a terrible storm blew

up. The Mulla's crazy cockleshell was filling with water. He leaned over toward his companion.

"Have you ever learned to swim?"

"No," said the pedagogue.

"In that case, schoolmaster, all your life is lost, for we are sinking."[1]

The two characters in the story are representative of two modes of consciousness. They are complementary; each has its function and a whole person has fully developed both modes. Yet in both religious and secular education we have tended to separate the active (intellectual) and the receptive (intuitive) modes of consciousness, emphasizing one over the other. Technological knowledge plays a dominant influence in our culture. Largely analytical, verbal, linear, and rational, it has tended to deemphasize and devalue other modes of consciousness. Its concern for verbal, intellectual knowledge, and its focus upon planning, organizing, and doing, have served to screen out other sorts of knowledge and life.

Edward Hall in his book, *The Hidden Dimension,* provides us with insight into how we all screen in and out particular knowledge. He explains that people brought up in different cultures learn as children, without ever knowing that they have done so, to screen out one set of experiences and pay close attention to another. Consider, for example, that in the Arctic there is no horizon separating earth and sky. Visibility in the snow is all but nonexistent, yet the Eskimo can travel across miles of such terrain because of an awareness of the relationship between contours, types of snow, wind, salt air, and ice cracks. However, the same Eskimo would most likely find it difficult to travel confidently through the streets of New York City. While such cultural screening may be necessary and helpful, other sorts of screening may not.

Each of us arrives in the natural world as an unfinished product. Within the limits of nature, we collectively build a human world in which we can live and grow. Through largely unconscious means we are socialized into valuing particular modes of consciousness, thereby determining our understanding of the world. Our culture has tended to place a greater value on one mode of consciousness—the intellectual. Our educational programs in both church and society have focused, therefore, upon verbal, analytical, logical, thinking skills. At least, that is the thesis behind Jerome Bruner's important book, *On Knowing: Essays for the Left Hand*.

The bankruptcy of this one-sided emphasis is dramatically expressed in Herman Hesse's great novel on education. *Beneath the Wheel* is at once a story of Hesse's own experience and an attack on any educational system that fosters intellectual development at the expense of intuition. I suggest that it is the artificial separation of these two modes of consciousness and the overemphasis on the intellect that has crippled us as a people and limited our spiritual development. Religious education, by mirroring general education and reflecting the culture's dominant concern for the intellect, has neglected the intuitional mode of consciousness and, therefore, I contend it has not provided learning necessary for the life of prayer.[2]

The depreciation of the signative, conceptual, and analytical aspects of human life and the benign neglect of the symbolic, mythical, imaginative, and emotive aspects have limited our spiritual development and crippled us as a people. A whole person living the spiritual life has developed fully both the receptive and active modes of consciousness. However, a new awareness of the visual, artistic, imaginative, associative, and relational activities of the brain cannot be permitted to dull or limit our concern for speech, logic, cognitive reasoning, analysis, and linear activities. The religious life of activity and the interior life of experience must be united. Christian spirituality has a symbolic-signative, mythic-conceptual, imaginative-analytical, informational-emotive character. Inherent in every individual, intense, interior religious experience is the passionate need to creatively express socially, through word and deed, the wholeness of life. Correspondingly, every verbal expression or behavioral act shared in community has a passionate need to secure itself in the world of depthful, transcendent experience, ritual, and myth. We humans are created in the image of God. We are, therefore, historical actors. Our wills, to be Christian, need to unite intellect and intuition into ethical activity in our personal and social history. That is what it means to live the spiritual life. The ideal is St. Teresa of Avila who combined piety, religious ecstasy, and politics, or institutional reform.

In the year 1515, Teresa, a child of Spanish aristocracy, was born in a palace in Avila. Educated by Augustinian nuns, at fifteen she entered a Carmelite monastery. Shortly thereafter a mysterious paralyzing illness obliged her to return to her family, but on her recovery she reentered the convent. There she led a typically lax moral life, enjoyed a well-appointed suite, entertained friends, and regularly left the cloister to visit aristocratic ladies. Her behavior was not uncommon, for an endemic sickness of the soul and moral laxity existed throughout the church. It was a difficult time to be nurtured into Christian faith and life, and most people succumbed to the world's ways.

However, in 1555, at the age of forty, while praying before a statue of Christ, Teresa experienced a conversion, a transformation, a falling in love, and a subsequent opening of her eyes and ears to that which lies beyond the boundaries of our knowing. From that moment on, her prayers brought her into God's very presence. Divine locutions, visions, and ecstasy followed. The life of perfection beckoned and as a faithful response she determined to find a house where disciplined contemplation and the single rule of life would be strictly observed.

In the face of strong opposition from both church and state, she single-handedly began to carry out her plan. In 1562 she founded the monastery of St. Joseph of Avila and wrote her first book, *The Way of Perfection*.

The subsequent years were filled with both contemplation and labor. Facing one difficulty after another, she built, reformed, and restored numerous convents and priories. At the same time her religious life deepened through prayer and, at the last she accepted the responsibility of being prioress at Avila where she wrote *Foundations for Life*, and at age sixty-seven she peacefully died.

St. Teresa was a woman of strong character, shrewdness, and great practical ability. As a writer, her influence was epoch-making. The combination of mystic religious experience with ceaseless prophetic activity as writer, reformer, and organizer makes her a classical instance for the contention that the highest contemplation is not incompatible with great practical achievement; in fact the two go together, each supporting and embracing and necessary, I might add, for the other.

We humans are spiritual beings. Our human spirituality has not dried up. Dimensions of our spirituality have been suppressed but not destroyed. Eventually they will emerge and seek to express themselves, for the human spiritual quest is the natural drive of persons to become human in the fullest sense.

Observations

Over the years, I have observed a host of persons engaged in religious education. The majority were faithful, caring, committed persons; some were exceptional teachers; a few were engaged in truly creative learning experiences with children. In most cases, however, learning tasks were controlled by teachers who were primarily concerned with the mastery of cognitive skills and the direct transmission of information, facts, or concepts. Creative activities, if used at all, were supplementary. A heavy reliance on verbal material prevailed. Control and discipline were valued, while teachers typically felt they were expected to follow rigidly prepared courses of study. I found that little time was devoted to experiential activities, discovery, curiosity, or spontaneity. Silence, wonder, and creative expression were only rarely encouraged. Teachers, like the parents of the children they taught, were concerned that children acquire "basic knowledge." There was, therefore, much emphasis on subject matter, knowing, thinking, and analytical skills.

Recently I observed religious educators dealing with prayer. Some were quite imaginative in their teaching, yet prayer was most often understood as a subject to be mastered. Teachers emphasized the nature of prayer, how to pray, when to pray, why to pray, where to pray, and what to pray for. Once again, I witnessed little learning focused upon wonder, awe, mystery, or surprise. Few teachers seemed concerned for the senses: seeing, hearing, smelling, tasting, or touching. Dreaming, imagining, creating, wondering, fantasizing, or envisioning were rarely the primary aims of their lessons. In most cases the children did not notice. A few, if they had been encouraged, might have cried out with Albert Cullum:

Teacher let us swim in a puddle
Let us race a cloud in the sky;
Let us build a house without walls,
But most of all
Let me laugh at nothing things.[3]

Yet most were content, happy, and interested, for those children who hoped for different sorts of learning had already dropped out.

Nevertheless, a good deal of significant change has taken place in religious education during the past decade. Many previous negative judgments need to be tempered. My remarks should not be misunderstood as another critical attack on those who have dedicated their lives to the difficult and awesome task of religious education. My point is simply this: While many creative teaching methods are being employed, religious education is primarily focused on the discovery of the general, the universal, and the abstract, rather than on the idiosyncratic, the concrete, and the experiential. Learning in religious education, in spite of many exciting innovations, is still dominantly verbal, conceptual, and analytic. The development of the intellect is primary. Little attention is given to intuition and the affections. The price to be paid for this educational imbalance is great: it may be making learning to pray difficult.

Participation in the arts as well as more structured opportunities for effective learning will be necessary. Catechesis must not shy away from sense-awareness exercises, imagination games, contemplation, or fantasy experiences; nor from the use of drama, dance, music, and the plastic arts. Concern for the affections ought once again to become a central component of all educational programs with children, youth, and adults. No longer can we permit persons to neglect the touch, smell, or taste of life; to escape the expressing of feelings; or to avoid creative expression through the use of the arts.

However, a rebirth of concern for the affections and the nurture of the intuitive mode of consciousness is not enough. As long as we continue our present educational practices, which neglect the development of an historicist perspective, true Christian prayer will avoid us. Therefore, I suggest, we need to focus on the development of historical awareness.

That will not be easy. We live in an historical time. People seem to have been taught history as a meaningless collection of dates, names, and places. Few are conscious of a meaningful past, and most consider the past they do recall as irrelevant to the present. As a result, many are trapped in the present. Without a critical, appreciative, personal consciousness of the past there is no vision of the future. Indeed the present itself takes on meaning in the light of an awareness which affirms the relevance of the past.

The Judeo-Christian faith is founded upon an historicist perspective. Within the cumulative tradition of the Judeo-Christian faith, God is understood as one who acts —to create the world and all creatures, to sustain the world through interaction with those creatures according to "his" purposes, and to bring the world and all "she" has made to the ends for which "he" created them. God, in the Judeo-Christian story, is an incarnate agent who acts on and in the world. History is, therefore, intentional and directional. Through God's revelatory historical actions we understand the past, gain hope for the present and a vision of the future. Our lives, and indeed life itself, takes on meaning and purpose in the light of that story.

The significance of the biblical understanding of God as the one who acts is founded upon an understanding of the whole course of history; that is, history which is ordered toward God's ultimate goal—"her" kingdom. With the ultimate goal of history as our vision, we can understand the present and interpret the past. Religious education, therefore, ought to focus on helping persons to live in and for God's kingdom, to live in the light of a hoped-for future and to understand their place in life as essentially historical agents committed to fulfilling themselves through the exercise of their wills in reflective action.

To accomplish these goals we will need to consider how persons acquire their perspective or view of the world. Gordon Kaufman suggests that we relate to the world in one or more ways: through thinking, feeling, and acting.[4] Each approach to experience results in a particular way of viewing the world. A dominance of thinking tends to issue forth in a "secular" world view, a view which ignores the depth of reality, our need to be at one with the world, and desire for insight about the future. Kaufman also suggests that when feeling is given a dominant place in shaping our understanding of life, a "religious" world view results. Such a view of the world, while affirming the importance of the the affections, neglects the moral dimensions of our volitional life. Only when we make action the dominant mode of our world viewing do we establish what Kaufman describes as a "theistic" world view, a perspective which speaks of a reality other than humanity and the world: "Theism takes the world to be ordered from beyond itself by intentional and purposeful activity rooted in the will of God."[5] Life according to this latter world view is understood as derivative from God and his purposes as revealed in "his" historical action. Each of us is a thinking, feeling, willing self. For too long we have either emphasized our thinking or feeling natures in religious education. We need to reemphasize our lives as praxis—willing, passionate, reflective action.

Most agree that faith is a free, centered act of the whole personality, but faith is typically understood either as knowing (cognition), as a personal relationship or trust (affections), or as obedient action (volition). The first fosters a detached contemplation on God, the search for wisdom, and as submission to revealed doctrine and right thinking. The second places emphasis on a lively personal relationship with God. And the third focuses upon reflective action with God in the world.

To complicate matters, in the English language faith is a noun, a word that refers or points to something else —a person, place, or thing. If we think of faith as a thing, we can easily say that we have "found it" or "lost it." From this point of view, faith is a possession understood as personal salvation, spirit (joy in the Lord), a resource for personal living, or knowledge. But it is more hopeful to think of faith as a centered integrated action, as a verb. We should speak of "being faithful" rather than of "having faith." Speaking of being faithful rightly emphasizes the integration of thinking, feeling, and willing. Faith is a matter of who we are, of how we think, and of what we do in response to what God does for us and how God acts in history. For this understanding of faith to take shape in our lives, we need also to develop an historical consciousness.

Such an historicist perspective is encouraged by participation in the life of a history-bearing community of faith whose past is made present and personal. Too often, if we have told our story at all, we have told it as if it were a series of separate past events with a minimum of personal significance. For example, we recall how God is said to have once upon a time freed some Israelites from bondage in Egypt. How much more significant to recall that God freed us in our bondage once, continues to free us, and will free us at last at the end of time.

H. Richard Niebuhr[6] wrote of the distinction between our history and events in impersonal time, between history as lived and history as contemplated from the outside. To illustrate, he contrasted the *Cambridge Modern History:* "On July 4, 1776, Congress passed the resolution which made the colonies independent communities, issuing at the same time the well-known Declaration of Independence, . . ." with Lincoln's Gettysburg Address: "Four-score and seven years ago our fathers brought forth upon this continent a new nation, conceived in liberty and dedicated to the proposition that all men are created equal." Too often we have taught the history of our faith like the *Cambridge Modern History.* The result has been to prevent a development of an historical consciousness.

If we continue to place our emphasis in religious education on doctrine (what persons ought to believe) or on the Bible (sacred literature to be learned about), we will continue to make that historicist perspective, which is necessary for prayer, difficult to acquire. Instead we need to consider directing our educational efforts toward storytelling. We need to transmit in meaningful ways the story of our faith, the story of God's historical acts in the lives of his/her people. From the earliest years, in the context of a celebrating faith community, children, youth, and adults need to experience the faith story through song, dance, drama, and the visual arts. Classrooms should be avoided for they tend to structure experience in ways which cause us to teach *about* our history. It would be better to return to the fireside and supper table where we can recall ways and dramatically retell the story of the mighty acts of God, and to our houses of worship where through preaching and celebration we can communicate the acts of God and our vision of God's kingdom. It will be necessary for us to learn "our story" in ways that make the past part of the present and future. We must once again become a storytelling people. We need to seek ways to communicate *the* story as *our* story, ways to express it through word and deed and ways to use it as our foundation for reflective action. Most of all we need to frame our lives in community so that we are significantly engaged in reflective action as a story-living people. When we have become involved in that sort of religious education, we will have begun to lay the foundations for the Christian life of prayer.

Catechesis, then, needs to aid in the full growth of an historical awareness and the integration of our receptive and active modes of consciousness. Only then will ritual prayer—the symbolic actions of the faith community—have power and meaning for us. Only when daily prayer (our conscious awareness of God's presence in our personal and social history) is a natural part of our lives will ritual prayer be purposeful. We do not proceed from ritual prayer to prayer; it is the other way around. Good rituals express and telescope our experience. Without experience, rituals remain dead forms. Without radically changed educational programs neither prayer nor ritual prayer can have significance in our individual or corporate lives.

The road to reforming our educational programs and our corporate lives as celebrating, experiencing, acting communities of faith will be long and hard. But the reward is worth all struggles, for it is only through a changed consciousness that the world will be transformed. True revolution is revelation. Prayer is thus at the heart of the Christian revolution, for true prayer necessitates a change of consciousness. Reformed and renewed catechesis can make a significant contribution to that cause, while the continuation of our present program will only make the life of prayer, indeed the Christian life, increasingly difficult.

Two and a half centuries ago a struggle emerged within the faculty of Saint Thomas's School in Leipzig, an unresolved struggle which still marks a schism in the soul of the church. It was a conflict between the intellectual and intuitional modes of consciousness, the struggle between the school's cantor, Johann Sebastian Bach, and its rector, Johann August Ernesti. Ernesti, a pioneer in the literary, historical, critical study of the Scriptures, believed the students should study more and sing less; Bach thought faith and its musical expressions more important. As Jan Chiapusso, the biographer of Bach, put it: "Here we see the tragic conflict between the last and most mighty musical representative of the age of faith and the younger protagonist of the age of reason and science."[7] Two epics, two cultures, two understandings were at stake. Ernesti wished to make the study of religion the sole purpose of the school. Bach tried to defend the position that the biblical text was designed to release within the reader an intense sort of spiritual activity: faith. Ernesti chose religion—a rationalistic, analytical, intellectual perspective. Bach chose faith—an intuitional, experiential perspective. Since those days, the rationalists, with an emphasis on theological reflection and an interest in the literary, historical, critical method of biblical study, have dominated the church's intellectual life. While these scholars never won the people's hearts or had any great success in training the masses in their methods, they did influence our understandings and ways. However, it is not that their understandings and ways are unimportant; it is just that their shared emphasis on the intellectual mode of consciousness has contributed to the demise of intuition and the sickness of the spiritual life.

Revelation

Faith is a response experience to revelation. Revelation and faith belong together, just as theology and religion do. To speak of religion is to speak of institutions, documents, artifacts, customs, ceremonials, creedal statements, and codes of conduct. Faith on the other hand is deeply personal and dynamic. Faith is a centered act of the total personality. Faith is not a result of a purely rational process. It is affectional, a relationship with God which embraces the whole person and about which it is difficult to be objective. To be sure, faith always expresses itself in religion and, as such, religion provides us with the means by which we grow in faith. Religion is a witness to and stimulant of faith. Religion is never an end, only a means; faith is an end. For example, Bach wrote his *B Minor Mass* as an expression of his faith. Whenever I sing or hear the *B Minor Mass* I am moved to faith, but to know all about the *B Minor Mass* is of little significance for faith. The Nicene Creed, Augustine's theology, and the Heidelberg Catechism are all expressions of faith. My faith is aided by these doctrinal statements, but they are examples of religion, and to make them the focus of our attention is to ignore the issue of faith. Surely, there is a difference between learning about the Heidelberg Catechism and being a faithful disciple of Jesus Christ; there is a difference between learning about the doctrine of salvation and being saved; there is a difference between understanding justification by faith and being justified by it; there is a difference between understanding religion and religious experience and having an experience of God's presence. Faith is not knowledge about, or even intellectual ascent to, truth or ideas. It is a response to a person.

Revelation refers to those actions of God to which we respond in faith. For too long theology has been emphasized, though never fully accepted, as an intellectual body of doctrine to be conserved and transmitted. Revelation is a different matter. God does not reveal truths about God's self. God reveals God's self. Through God's actions God communicates and relates. Revelation affects our consciousness and re-creates us. It transforms our relationships to self, neighbor, and world. Revelation is best understood as a personal encounter with a living, acting God. Revelation, therefore, is essentially a relationship with God, not a set of doctrines, ideas about the world, or new knowledge.

Theology is doctrine. It is a natural consequence of revelation, just as religion is a natural consequence of faith. Revelation, however, is always prior and therefore foundational to the spiritual life. For example, the message of eternal life is not essentially information about another world, but first and foremost the Word of God's presence in creating life out of death. Our lives can be shattered by sickness, failure, or accident. We are all vulnerable to forces beyond our control. Still the good news is that in every experience of death God is present transforming it into life. For those who have experienced this revelation there is reason to reflect upon it and to express it theologically. Being aware of the resulting doctrinal formulations can even aid us to better understand our experience. But revelation, as a relational experience of God, is what is of primary importance.

Never was this truth made clearer than in a story told by a colleague. It seems that one of his academic friends was critically ill, paralyzed, incontinent of bowel and bladder, and unable to speak. There he was, helpless in a hospital bed, wanting to communicate but unable to do so. My friend, an Episcopal priest, went to see him. The man's wife sat helpless at his side. The priest stood by him, held his hand, and said, "I know you want to speak and can't. I also know that you would want me to sign you with the cross, and that is why I came." As he put his thumb to the man's forehead, the bowel and bladder of the helpless man emptied itself. The odor filled the air, and his wife, in despair and with tears in her eyes, exclaimed, "Oh, why did he have to do that now?" And my colleague responded, "What better time to acknowledge that you have no control over your life than when you are being signed with the cross?" Revelation! The presence of God bringing life out of death—not ideas about God confined to the intellect but a relationship involving the world of intuition.

We need to revolt against the objective consciousness so that we might regain our mystical sensibilities. Ultimately, the only authority for faith is the Word of God, the activity of God, the revelation of God, the Word made flesh in Jesus Christ. The Bible, as the story of the relationship between God and God's people, is an approximate authority. And so, importantly, is contemporary personal experience. Scripture and experience must judge the tradition; Scripture and the tradition judge experience; tradition and experience judge the Scriptures; while all are judged by the final authority upon which the community of faith rests: God's action in Jesus Christ. Theology, at its best, is a process of thinking, of reflecting on revelation—the relationship that God initiates with God's people in every age, and which can and needs to be experienced again in our own. However, neither Scripture, tradition, nor experience can become revelation—God's Word—without the operation of the intuitional mode of consciousness. That is, we only experience this relationship with God metaphorically. We do not have direct experiences of God; no one has seen God. But neither do we know God essentially through ideas.

A metaphorical, poetic, symbolic, mythical relationship to God is always prior to any signative, conceptual, analytical relationship. Our ideas about God are important. Indeed, they can influence the sort of experiences of God we have and do not have. In one sense then, our revelation of God is made possible through the ideas of God which are passed on through the tradition. But that is only a partial truth. Our experiences frame and form our ideas. People in the first century experienced the resurrected Christ and his presence at the breaking of the bread. Their ideas about God and God's coming community were framed by that relational experience, which, metaphorically, we communicate each time we celebrate the Lord's Supper. To become aware of God's continuing revelation is to nurture the intuitional mode of consciousness.

For too long we have been living in the prosaic world of surface reality. We need to affirm the poetic truth of metaphor and myth by questioning the basic premise of the naturalistic universe and social science's search for clear explanations. Perhaps the true explanations of life are beyond concepts, to be reached only through the intuition. Human intellect may never comprehend the full set of causes preceding any situation, consequence, or feeling. We need to repeal the fundamental law of cause and effect which has been an unquestioned statute since the Enlightenment. It is important for the spiritual life that we replace the sole rule of linear, logical, rationalistic thinking and return to the earlier age of mystery, which held sway before the advent of Newtonian physics, Cartesian logic, and behavioral psychology.

One of the early representations of Christ in Christian art depicts a crucified human figure with the head of an ass. The debate on its meaning continues, but I am convinced that these catacomb Christians had a deep sense of the comic absurdity of their position. A wretched band of slaves, derelicts, and square pegs, they must have sensed how ludicrous their claims appeared. The revelation they announced, lived and died for, was irrational and illogical. For them Christ must have seemed something of a holy fool, and they knew that they were fools for Christ. More important, they had faith and hope in the eternal foolishness of God. To have faith in the revelation of God in Jesus Christ is to live in the ludicrous world of imagination, poetry, and metaphor. As Herbert Marcuse, I believe once said, "We need to break the power of facts over the world and speak a language which is not the language of those who establish, enforce and benefit from the facts." To live in and for the Gospel is to be a godly fool, a laughing stock for the Word of God.

Our faith experiences are always translated (and need to be) into religious beliefs. This process of institutionalization involves the symbolic transformation of the experience of God into less than ultimate forms. While this bringing of the sacred into profane structures is necessary, it provides a dilemma for the church. Since the faith experience of revelation is spontaneous and creative, the necessary institutionalization of revelation reduces such experience.

Myth

One way to maintain the significance of revelation is to remind ourselves of the centrality of myth. Myths provide the foundations for our rituals and the means for expressing God's revelation. More important, they point to and participate in the spiritual dimension of life. Unfortunately myth has been erroneously understood as distinct from reality, possessing only a pretense at historical reliability. Regretfully, this understanding of myth has caused Christians, whose faith is based upon God's historical actions, to consider myth to be irrelevant. The faith of the church rests upon the biblical record of God's history-making, especially upon a particular historical person, Jesus Christ, and his actual death and resurrection. Some contend that while the Gospel is not myth, it had to be set forth in the form of myth in order to reach the depths of human consciousness in the first century. Therefore, they conclude, it is necessary to de-mythologize the Bible in order to discover its true significance and/or to make it speak to modern, secular, urban humans who cannot understand or appreciate its mythical form. I simply want to go on record as not accepting either of these latter contentions. Myth can be understood by moderns. More importantly, it is essential to the spiritual life of the Christian. The attempt to de-mythologize the Scriptures may not be as important as was once thought. Myths have their life in the symbolic and are therefore best understood through the intuitional mode of consciousness.

The Pawnee, an American Indian tribe, differentiated between true and false stories. True stories were about the sacred; false stories about the profane. True stories are myths: they are stories because they recount events that really took place, that is, they are not fiction or fable but history; however, they are true because they recount sacred history. Profane stories only explain our historical events. Sacred stories, myths, point beyond their historical roots to the dimension of depth, of the transcendent, in history. They are true not in the sense of logic or intellectual analysis, but in terms of mystery and intuition. Myth unites history with the sacred, giving it particular symbolic significance in the lives of people. The story of the life, death, and resurrection of Jesus is on the one hand a profane, historical account, but it is also much more. It is a sacred story, myth, because it points beyond its historicity to the cosmic action of God in the salvation of the world. To demythologize the story is to lose its dimension of depth and significance.

Myths are never told for their own sake or as a means of expressing intellectual doctrines. They are a mode of expression which as symbolic narrative transmit the truths only the intuition can grasp and understand. There are various sorts of knowledge; each has its own significance and character. Scientific, rational knowledge is only one kind. The Scripture contains the sacred myths of Christian community. They ought not to be reduced to rational discourse. The Bible is poetry plus, not science minus. Our myths communicate the revelation of God and sustain the understandings and ways of the faithful. For too long we have attempted to understand reality solely through reason and have forgotten the importance of symbolic narrative, metaphor, and sacred story. Christianity is a historical, but also a metaphorical religion. In our culture, we have lost our intuitional power to grasp the truth of myth because we have canonized historic and scientific positivism. Nevertheless, we no more live in a post-mythical age than we live in a post-intuitional age, except in the sense that our intuitional mode of consciousness has atrophied.

Ritual

Liberal Protestants, in particular, but also some Roman Catholic liberals, have tended to put more emphasis on political and economic social action than on corporate symbolic action—ritual—forgetting that ritual is necessary to support, inspire, and sustain significant social action over time. And, perhaps even more important, our rituals themselves either encourage or discourage political and social action. The result has been disastrous. While the church in general, nurtured by otherworldly, individualistic rituals, has denied the importance of political, economic, and social action, those most committed to a this-worldly, social understanding of the faith have typically left the church or at least stopped participating in its rituals. In our quest for historical relevance and faithfulness, we have forgotten that ritual is at the heart of all social change.

It is not so much in rational planning as in the imagination that the world is changed. We live by our images and dreams. As Amos Wilder once wrote, "It is in the area of liturgics—the idiom and metaphor of prayer and witness—that the main impasse lies today for the Christian."[8]

Ritual is a social drama which embodies the memories and visions of a community. It is through the repetition of these symbolic actions that we evoke the feeling of the primordial event which initially called the community into being, with such power that it effects a present presence at that event. In other words, through the intuitional mode of consciousness, ritual re-presents revelation. An example would be the Christian ritual of baptism or the Lord's Supper, both of which re-present the event of Jesus' death and resurrection.

This truth took on significance one night a number of years ago when I was in Paraguay. A political prisoner had escaped from prison and told me about his celebration of Easter two days before. It appears that the prisoners had been forbidden to worship, but while the non-Christians kept the guards busy, the Christians huddled together. The pastor, also a prisoner, began: "This meal in which we are part, reminds us of the prison, the torture, the death, and the final victory and resurrection of

Jesus Christ. He asked us to remember him by repeating this action in the spirit of fellowship. The bread which we do not have today, but which is present in the spirit of Jesus Christ, is the body which he gave for humanity. The fact that we have none represents very well the lack of bread and the hunger of so many millions of human beings. When Christ distributed bread among his disciples, and when he fed the people, he revealed the will of God that we should all have bread. The wine which we do not have today is his blood present in the light of our faith. Christ poured it out for us to move us toward freedom in the long march for justice. God made all persons of one blood: The blood of Christ represents our dream of a unified humanity, of a just society without difference of race or class."

The pastor then told of a man of about sixty whose daughter had died fighting with the guerrillas, who said, "I think this communion means that our dead are alive, that they have given their bodies and blood, making Christ's sacrifice their own. I believe in the resurrection of the dead and feel their presence among us." There was silence and the pastor continued: "This communion is not only a communion between us here, but a communion with all our brothers and sisters in the church or outside, not only those who are alive, but those who have already died. Still more, it is a communion with those who will come after us and who will be faithful to Jesus Christ."

The prisoner then told how the pastor held out his empty hands to each person, placing his hand over theirs as they together boldly exclaimed, "Take, eat, this is my body which is given for you, do this in remembrance of me. Take, drink, this is the blood of Christ which was shed to seal the new covenant of God with humanity. Let us give thanks, sure that Christ is here with us, strengthening us." Then they raised their hands to their mouths and received the body and blood of Christ and, after sharing the kiss of peace, they returned to their life in prison with new hope.

Through the power of symbolic actions we order our experience; through the use of symbolic narrative we explain our lives. Ritual operates on those levels of existential reality that undergird the conceptual. More importantly, ritual points to and participates in that primordial truth which is located at the expanding edge of our horizon of knowing, in feeling and intuition, not in common sense or thinking. Just as it is the language of myth, which at the most fundamental level enables us to perceive reality, so it is in our symbolic actions—our rituals—and our social dramas that we experience the ultimate meanings and purposes of life and our lives. Without ritual life becomes mundane and profane, for it is through ritual expressive of the symbolic and founded in the intuitive mode of consciousness that the sacramental and the sacred are best known and expressed.

When we participate in a ritual, we experience community, we reconcile and identify ourselves with our foreparents from whom the ritual has descended, and we reestablish continuity with the past and vision for the future.

Ritual is drama; it is life in the world of the receptive mode of consciousness. When our intuition atrophies, our rituals lose their power. Correspondingly, meaningful ritual can enhance and enliven our intuitional mode of consciousness. Unless, therefore, ritual is raised to its proper significance, our spiritual lives will remain impotent.

Throughout the history of the Christian church two understandings of the religious or spiritual life have been pitted against one another. Which is it to be: the contemplative worship of the divine or the active service of the human, religious experience or prophetic action, piety or politics, mystic enlightenment or social responsibility, an ecstatic union with God or a good deed for the neighbor, prayer or witness?

Are we humans best understood as *homo faber* or *homo politicus?* Is the receptive, the intuitive, the interior, the experiential-relational or the active, the intellectual, the external, the reflection-action mode of consciousness more significant? Is religion housed in the affections, the realm of subjective experience or in the will, the realm of rational interpretation and objective action? Who are we, and what is it to have life and have it abundantly?

These questions and their implications have haunted the church's educational ministry from time immemorial. Once again they have surfaced. A decade ago it was education for social change. Today it is education for spirituality. Advocates of various positions abound. Each wisely gives a nod to the other pole and then proceeds to emphasize the essential nature of his own bias. Few are able to maintain any sort of dynamic balance or interrelatedness.

My contention is that catechesis—the pastoral ministry of the church concerned that divine revelation be made known, that faith be enhanced and enlivened, and that persons and the community be prepared for their vocation in the world—is best understood as supporting the paradox of the absolute, though seemingly incompatible, nature of both modes of consciousness and their necessary complementarity for the spiritual life of the Christian.

Let us review again our understanding of these two paradoxical modes of consciousness. The active mode is the intellectual-volitional mode. It includes the signative, conceptual, analytical, organizational aspects of reality. It is the word of speech, logic, reason, planning, decision-making, and doing. It is characterized by external life in the polis. It is the world of structure and cosmos.

The receptive mode is the intuitive mode. It includes the symbolic, mythic, imaginative, creative, emotive dimensions of reality. It is the world of visions and dreams, of aesthetic, experiential, wholistic, relational activity. It is characterized by the interior life. It is the world of antistructure and chaos. These two modes are polar opposites, each demanding loyalty, each asserting its ultimacy and each insufficient without the other. Nevertheless, each is necessary for the health of the other and both are necessary for the wholeness of human life.

As Thomas Merton wrote, "He who attempts to act and do things for others without deepening his own self understanding, freedom, integrity, and capacity to love will not have anything to give others. He will communicate to them nothing but the contagion of his own obsession, his aggressiveness, his ego-centered ambition, his delusions about ends and means, his doctrines and prejudices."[9] Similarly, as the author of the Letter of James put it, ". . . if the experience of God does not lead to action it is itself a lifeless thing" (2:17). Needless to say, that may explain why the commandment reads, "You are to love God with all your heart, soul and mind and you are to love your neighbor as yourself" (Matt. 22:37–38).

The spiritual life of the Christian is the interior life of devotion to God and to the exterior life of prophetic acts on behalf of the good of all humanity. A Christian conscience is an activity of the whole person in devotion to Jesus Christ as Lord, making judgments on what is faithful and acting accordingly. It is in the world of liturgy that the spiritual life is realized. It is in the world of catechesis that our liturgical life is reformed, enhanced, and enlivened.

The church as a community of faith is our parent and teacher, nurturing and instructing us in Christian faith. The church provides the most important context for the formation and transformation of human life. As St. Augustine wrote, "I would not have believed the Gospel if the authority of the church (its holiness of life and faithfulness of witness) had not moved me." The church, catholic and reformed, needs to begin to understand liturgy as primarily and fundamentally a way of daily individual and corporate life in the world. We are called to live the Eucharist day by day, hour by hour. Liturgy understood as our ritual symbolic actions needs to nurture, sustain, and inspire our intellects, intuitions, and behaviors in ways consistent with the Gospel. Inadequate rituals will only lead to inadequate lives.

If, therefore, we are concerned about the spiritual life, we need first to introduce into both our churches and schools ways of learning which enable persons to develop the receptive, intuitional, nonverbal, emotional modes of consciousness as well as the intellectual and volitional. And second, we need to introduce into our common life ways of learning which encourage the growth of an historical consciousness and perspective on life. Accepting these two aims for catechesis will mean radical changes both in our educational programs and in our corporate lives as faith communities. But if we are truly concerned about the Christian spiritual life, I believe we have no option.

·7·

Christian Initiation:
Nurture and Conversion

Initiation rites, as studied by anthropologists, comprise ritual actions and oral teachings which result in decisive changes in a person's religious and social status and role. Typically, through a series of ordeals, people learn the ways and the understandings of the adult community, encounter the sacred, experience death and rebirth, and emerge as new persons whose existence in the community is significantly transformed.

Historically, initiation plays an essential role in practically every known religion. Indeed, it appears that we only fully understand and are committed to religious truth insofar as we are initiated into it by acts of personal faith or conversion symbolically dramatized through ritual. Elaborate incorporation rites, by which Christians became full members of the church, were characteristic of the first four centuries of the Christian era. Wrapped in secrecy, after weeks of intense preparation, these rites were calculated to inspire religious experience and celebrate the occasion for a profound conversion. Initiation lies at the core of all genuine life, but in the modern western world significant initiation rites are practically nonexistent. However, to understand those incorporation rites which have survived in contemporary Protestant churches, it is necessary to differentiate between: (1) Faith commitment incorporation rites through which persons witness to personal faith, and (2) Institutional incorporation initiation rites through which persons join the church.

Faith commitment initiation rites appear most typical of those reported upon in the historical and comparative study of religion. The Christian church during the first three centuries is a good example. Vestiges of this understanding still persist in some churches, but institutional incorporation rites appear most typical of contemporary mainline Protestant churches. The report which follows demonstrates this contention. It was a result of a research project conducted on United Methodist and African Methodist Episcopal churches in the South.

United Methodists

One of the largest mainline Protestant denominations in the United States, the United Methodist Church traces its history to the eighteenth-century Church of England and John Wesley. Typically, the Methodists in our study define the church in terms of its institutional members, that is, those who have officially united with a church. The primary expectations of members are twofold: to support financially the institution and to participate actively in its organizational life. Only holding office where institutional and organizational decisions are made and the right to vote on matters of church finance and business are restricted to members. Nonmembers may teach in the church school and hold offices in all other church clubs and organizations. Church offices and institutionally important roles are most often restricted to members who have the greatest economic and social status in the community.

In the United Methodist churches studied, a lengthy rite of incorporation, called baptism, typically begins with a ritual for children, sometimes during their first two years, and is consummated for adolescents between ten and thirteen years of age, with a ritual known officially as confirmation but most often referred to as "the reception of new members" or "joining the church."

The significance of baptism is most often described as making a person a "preparatory member." An eight-to-thirteen-year period follows during which a child is nurtured and instructed in the church's understandings and ways. The rite is finally completed by a ritual marking full membership in the church. However, it must be noted that persons who "join the church" in adolescence are denied many of the rights and privileges of full membership until the legal age of eighteen.

Functionally, baptism announces that the institution has claimed the child as one of its own. On one Sunday each year, as part of the regular Sunday ritual, parents are asked to bring their children, aged six months to three years, to be baptized. At the appropriate time, the parents come forward with their children and the minister announces the purpose of the ritual as spiritual, but the structure emphasizes initiation into potential church membership. For example, parents are asked the following questions: (1) Do you confess faith in Jesus Christ as Lord and Savior? (2) Do you accept the duty to bring up your child in that faith? and (3) Do you promise to keep your child under the ministry and guidance of the church until, by the power of God, he or she is brought to faith and confirmed as a full and responsible member of the church? But the emphasis is placed on the last question, and that is the question most people remember as being significant. Also, following the baptism of the child, the minister asks the congregation to affirm their commitment to bring up the child in the church.

The congregation meets this responsibility by providing formal programs of education. Attendance at a church school (typically called a Sunday School) is therefore considered essential for membership.

Once each year, on a date determined by the minister, an announcement of a "membership class" is made, and parents are asked to encourage their children to attend. Indeed, it is expected that all youth, usually at twelve or thirteen years, will participate. Youth whose parents are not related to the church are usually not recruited unless they have been active in the church school. Most youth brought up in the church do attend, and they appear to look forward to this event as a graduation from church school and an entry into adult church life.

Some form of special presentation in the form of instruction by the minister is required just prior to confirmation. These classes run anywhere from a one-hour session to weekly meetings for a full year. Most often, classes are conducted one hour a week for eight weeks and are called membership or pastor's classes. In these classes, information about the Bible, the church's history and beliefs, and the Christian way of life, which was to have been learned in the church school, is summarized.

Membership classes follow a schooling model with lectures, memorization, and sometimes exams. They are directed by the minister, who most often places a heavy emphasis on learning information about the church as an institution, especially Methodist history, polity, and practice, and the institutional responsibilities of church membership. Dedication to the Christian faith and life appear to be presupposed, and little or no attention is given to either the baptism vows made by the youth's parents or the vows to be taken at confirmation. While there are often lengthy rehearsals for this event, their intent is a smooth-running ceremony. More attention, therefore, is given to where people will stand and what they will do than to the questions they will be asked.

At a time designated by the minister, the confirmation ritual is held. Usually this ceremony is included in the regular Sunday morning ritual and is witnessed by all who attend. At the appropriate time the youth to be confirmed come forward dressed in their usual Sunday church attire. Having attended the preparatory classes, having stated a desire to become a member of the church and having been accepted by the minister for membership, they are asked to make public affirmation to five questions: (1) Do you renew the vows made at your baptism? (2) Do you confess Jesus Christ as your Lord and Savior and pledge allegiance to His Kingdom? (3) Do you receive and profess the faith contained in the Old and New Testament? (4) Do you promise to live a Christian life and remain a faithful member of the church? and (5) Will you be loyal to the United Methodist Church and uphold it by your prayers, presence, gifts, and service?

Interestingly, in every case examined, the last two questions appeared to be considered most important. Typically, the minister paused before asking these questions, spoke them more slowly and intently, looked the potential new members individually in the eyes and listened carefully for each response.

(On very rare occasions a child prepares for confirmation who has not been baptized. A ritual of baptism is then added prior to the confirmation service, but most often it appears to be rushed and considered of little importance.)

Following their vows, the candidates are asked to kneel. The minister puts his (her) hand on each one of their heads and prays that God will confirm them in Christian faith. The congregation then recites a formal welcome into the church and, as a reaffirmation of their confirmation vows, promises to also uphold the church by their prayers, presence, gifts, and service.

With that emphasis on institutional membership, the class of new members is asked to remain at the front of the sanctuary following the regular morning ritual in order that members of the congregation may greet them. Most often, however, only their parents and the older, more established leaders of the church, the institutional role models, do so.

Following this ritual, those confirmed will have their names added to the rolls of the church. Interestingly, however, they will be referred to as the "confirmation class" for another year and are most often not treated as full members of the church until later in life.

It needs to be mentioned at this point that there are other ways by which persons can become members of the church. Adults, those above the age of confirmation, can unite with the church in one of three ways: (1) affirmation of faith, for those who have never been confirmed, (2) reaffirmation of faith, for those who have been confirmed in a church that does not "transfer" members to the Methodist Church (such as the Roman Catholic Church), and (3) letter of transfer, for those who wish to switch from one Methodist church to another or from a Presbyterian church to a Methodist church. Since it is usual that most persons join the church in their youth, "letters of transfer" are the means by which most adults shift their membership from one congregation to another.

Institutional means of home visitations, coffee hours and socials, and participation in church organizations and groups are usually used to recruit adult members. Little preparation is given to adults, with the exception of those coming from another denomination. For these persons, the emphasis of their preparation is on Methodist history and polity. Ceremonies for these persons are held at the discretion of the minister, generally when a new group of members has been assembled. There is little difference in the form or nature of the ritual whether a person joins by affirmation of faith, reaffirmation of faith, or letter of transfer. In every case, the emphasis is on institutional loyalty and the continuation of active participation in the life of the church. While the official words used in the initiation rite refer to faith, the functional-structural nature of the rite and the understanding of the participants is institutional incorporation.

African Methodist Episcopal

A somewhat different incorporation rite was found among the members of the African Methodist Episcopal Church (AME). Dating from a late eighteenth-century split with the Methodist Church over racial issues, the African Methodist Episcopal Church represents the oldest black denomination in the United States. They define the church in terms of those who have confessed faith in Jesus Christ. A great deal of emphasis is placed on religious experience and public confession of faith. The primary expectation of members is that they will witness to their faith, and the major qualification of membership is the ability to describe a religious experience. Regardless of age or social status, all who make a public confession of faith are encouraged to assume leadership in the church, and all members may hold offices in the church or teach in the church school.

Therefore, while rites of incorporation in AME churches are much like those in United Methodist churches, the former churches have a number of unique characteristics. Like the United Methodist churches, it is customary to baptize babies. The significance of baptism, however, is most often described in terms of religious experiences and may take place prior to the morning worship service on any Sunday. Functionally, baptism marks the first step in a person's faith pilgrimage to religious experience. A sponsor (most often the child's grandparents, but sometimes another faithful member of the church; in either case an active church member), chosen by the parents, stands with them and promises to make sure that the child is nurtured in the faith.

The service begins when the minister publicly washes his hands. The infant is dressed in white, and the minister is assisted by a group of older women who have been selected deaconesses or stewardesses; they too are dressed in white. These stewardesses act as directors for the ceremony, arranging the people and giving instructions so that everyone can concentrate on the content of the ritual. The first act by the minister is a prayer asking that the child will experience grace and become a worthy member of the church. Then the minister gives the parents a charge and exhortation emphasizing the great responsibility they have to teach their children the beliefs of the church. The parents are directed to lead their children to the experience of faith by reading the Bible at home and by accompanying them to Sunday School and worship. The parents promise that they will do these things, and the minister baptizes the child. This act is followed by congregational singing, and morning worship continues.

Children and adults are usually found at both church worship and Sunday School, where the emphasis is upon learning the beliefs of the church and the importance of religious experience. The thrust of most every lesson is related to the importance of experiencing Christian faith and confessing that faith before the congregation. Between the ages of ten and twelve, such an experience is expected and most often occurs. While there is no formal ritual of confirmation or special preparation, children regularly attend the morning worship with their parents, and following each sermon the pastor makes a call for persons to come forward and confess their Christian faith. Individuals so moved come forward and are met by a steward or deacon of the church who asks their name and hears their confession of religious experience and faith. The candidate then faces the congregation and the steward recounts the person's testimony to a religious experience and presents this person to the minister who, in turn, presents him or her to the congregation. Members of the church joyfully come forward to offer the new members the right hand of fellowship; they make special positive notice of the new members' religious experiences and sometimes they recount their own. While the service continues, the new members and the steward leave so that the steward might briefly instruct the new members in the responsibilities of church membership and give them information on the African Methodist Episcopal Church. The emphasis of the service is on religious experience and witness to faith. The responsibilities of church membership are an afterthought.

The transfer of membership from another church is possible by following a similar procedure. During the call to religious experience and faith, these persons come forward and explain to the steward that they wish to transfer their membership and reaffirm their religious experience and faith. The steward explains this to the congregation and, as before, the congregation comes forward to greet them.

Members are recruited primarily through the Sunday worship services and the Sunday School program. More emphasis is placed on religious experience than on doctrine, and less emphasis is placed on institutional life.

While religious experience is the key for understanding church membership, we did not find emphasis on a single conscious conversion experience, more typical of denominations which have adult baptism. In the AME churches studied, nurture from baptism through early adolescence is expected to provide the necessary basis for religious experience so that a radical turning is not necessary. Nevertheless, the structural-functional nature of the African Methodist Episcopal Church's incorporation rite focuses upon a confession of faith and religious experience.

Conversion and Initiation

Few concepts are more vague and confusing to liberal mainline Protestants than conversion. Rarely have we used the word conversion, and all too frequently we have limited our concerns to membership campaigns. However, until we find a place for conversion within our educational ministry, the church's mission will remain impotent. Indeed, without converts, the church will have difficulty being a community of Christian nurture.

Evangelism, as I am using the word, refers to the process by which the Christian community of faith, through the proclamation of the Gospel in word and deed, leads persons inside and outside the church to a radical reorientation of life—conversion.

Evangelism is not indoctrination. It is testifying through transformed lives to the acts of God both within and without the community of faith. When we evangelize we witness through word-in-deed to the acts of God in Jesus Christ. Without this witness to the lordship of Christ, to the good news of God's new possibility, and to the Gospel's prophetic protest against all false religiousness, the church loses its soul and becomes an institution of cultural continuity maintaining the status quo, rather than an institution of cultural change living in and for God's coming community. Evangelism is best understood, therefore, as the means by which the church continually transforms its life and the lives of its people into a body of committed believers, willing to give anything and everything to the cause of historically mediating God's reconciling love in the world.

Christian faith goes counter to many ordinary understandings and ways of life. It is hardly possible for anything less than a converted, disciplined body to be the historical agent of God's work in the world. Christians are not born. Neither are they simply made, formed, or nurtured. Conversion—a reorientation of life, a change of heart, mind, and behavior—is a necessary aspect of mature Christian faith whether or not one grows up in the church.

The church can no longer surrender to the illusion that child nurture, in and of itself, can or will rekindle the fire of Christian faith either in persons or in the church. We have expected too much of nurture. We can nurture persons into institutional religion, but not into mature Christian faith. The Christian faith, by its very nature, demands conversion. We do not gradually educate persons to be Christian. To be Christian is to be baptized into the community of the faithful, but to be a mature Christian is to be converted.

Conversion implies the reordering of our perceptions, a radical change without which no further growth or learning is possible. Conversion, therefore, is not an end, but a new beginning. It is a reorientation of a person's life, a deliberate turning from indifference, indecision, doubt, or earlier form of piety to enthusiasm, conviction, illumination and new understandings and ways. Conversion is not solely a shift from no faith or another faith to

Christian faith; it is also an essential dimension in the life of all baptized, faithful, Christians.

Those who have been baptized as children and reared in the church also need to be converted. At some point all Christians must fully internalize the faith of the church and affirm their own faith by being confronted with the choice of whether or not they will accept or reject the authority of the Gospel. Incorporation into the Christian church requires that persons be brought to a personal life-transforming commitment to Christ. However, since Christian maturity and conversion never exist apart from human maturity, we ought not to impose the demands of adult faith and conversion on those who lack the prerequisites of human maturity.

Children and youth are Christians and members of the community of Christian faith by their baptisms. They are to be nurtured in this community's understandings and ways. They are also to be evangelized by God's transforming Word until in their maturity (adulthood) they experience a moment or period of conversion.

Commitment is neither a single occasion nor of a singular kind. In baptism our parents and the church make a commitment on our behalf. When we celebrate our first communion, we make a first commitment of faith and we declare our desire to participate in the life of a nurturing, tradition-bearing family. Later that commitment takes the strange and unsettling shape of personal doubt and struggle with the community of our nurture. Finally, in adulthood, following the experience of conversion, a new sense of personal commitment is realized. While not final, this commitment has the quality of a significant new start. Conversion, then, is best understood as a significant aspect of a long process in the growth and maturation of faith by Christians within the Christian family.

Thus, conversion(s) experienced by Christians nurtured within the community of faith do not characteristically happen in a moment, are not always sudden, dramatic, or emotional, though they may be all or any of these. Conversion(s) are best understood as a radical turning from "faith given" (through nurture) to "faith lived" (through conversion). Conversion(s) are radical because they imply internalization and the corresponding transformation of our lives. Conversion(s) are the result of the witness of the faithful and imply a turning from one style of faith, typical of children and adolescents, to another style of faith, possible for adults.

Authentic Christian life is personal and social life lived on behalf of God's reign in the political, social, and economic world. One cannot be nurtured into such a life —not in this world. Every culture strives to socialize persons to live in harmony with life as it is. The culture calls upon its religious institutions to bless the status quo, and it calls upon religion's educational institutions to nurture persons into an acceptance of life as it is.

But God calls "her" people to be signs of *shalom*, the vanguard of God's kingdom, a community of cultural change. To live in the conviction that such countercultural life is our Christian vocation in-but-not-of the world, necessitates conversion as well as nurture.

Once again, we need to understand that both conversion and nurture have a place in the church's educational ministry if it is to be Christian. Our sole concern for nurture has contributed to our losing both an evangelical power and a social dynamic. While rejecting a sterile revivalism, we constructed a false evangelism through nurture. True evangelism and conversion mean helping persons to see that they are called, not only to believe the church's affirmation that Jesus is the Christ but to commit their lives to him and to live as his apostles (witnesses) in the world.

Who but the converted can adequately nurture? And who but the nurtured can be adequately prepared for the radicalness of transformed life? Without the witness of Word and deed, which is the evangelical act, conversion cannot occur. Without nurture, the converted cannot adequately bear witness in the world. Unless conversion and nurture are united in the church's educational ministry, the church will have difficulty being the church of Jesus Christ, the bearer of the Gospel in the world.

What the church's educational ministry needs is a catechesis which evangelizes and an evangelism which catechizes. Nurture and conversion, conversion and nurture, belong together, taking different shapes and forms at various moments in a person's faith pilgrimage within the faith community.

The Christian life is continuous involving both experiences of formation (nurture) and transformation (conversions). Conversions begin at some point in time, but they are never completed. To speak of a conversion is to refer not only to an initial moment, no matter how revolutionary, but to the whole life of the believer in community. The gift of faith is something we are always learning. Conversions understood as process and multiple conversions throughout a persons life are basic to living faith. Healthy rituals must both convert and nuture us. They cannot become the means by which the church blesses and sustains the status quo of either individual or social life. We each need throughout our lives to be continually converted to deeper levels of faith.

Catechesis focuses on spiritual formation and the nurture of persons within a community of faith which, through its pastoral ministry, makes divine revelation known, enhances and enlivens faith, and prepares persons for their vocation. Evangelism focuses on spiritual transformation and the conversion of persons within a community of faith which, through its pastoral ministry, bears prophetic witness in word and deed to the presence of God's Word in history.

Evangelism proclaims and explains the Gospel so that faith might be aroused. Catechesis makes possible the growth and development of faith. The process is never-ending. Evangelism and catechesis, conversion and nurture, belong together. Christian initiation, the incorporation of persons into Christian life and mission requires both. Each is necessary for the other; when they are estranged, the church fails in its educational ministry. Today it is incumbent upon us to affirm the necessary paradox of catechesis and evangelism in the church's educational ministry and to reinterpret the nature and means of nurture and conversion within a community of faith. To the degree that we are successful, the Christian church will be faithful to its educational mission. In any case, Christian initiation cannot be understood apart from a discussion of conversion and ritual.

Learning and Change

Our rituals effectively influence human emotion and thought toward some behavioral purpose. Dead rituals are those which have lost their power to stimulate or evoke such experience. Initiation rituals are aimed primarily at the transformation of an individual's psychological orientation—conversion—in moving him or her from one place in the community to another. The ritual process of initiation needs to provide a significant detachment of the individuals from their present position or state in the community; an experience of liminality or in-between-ness; a psychic peak experience or conversion; and a reincorporation into the community as a new, "reborn" person.

Urban T. Holmes, Dean of the School of Theology, at

the University of the South, is one of our most important contemporary pastoral theologians. He has influenced my thought, and for many of my conclusions I am indebted to him. Recently he recounted to me the story of a priest studying for his doctorate at Marquette University where the thought of Bernard Lonergan has been very influential. On this occasion the priest was entertaining the German theologian Wolfhart Pannenberg. Pannenberg asked him, "Who is your principle mentor?" The reply was "Lonergan." "What a pity," Pannenberg remarked. "He is nothing but a pietist."

Now a pietist is a person who bases his beliefs on his inner feelings and often with a good bit of anti-intellectualism. So what did Pannenberg mean by this "put down" and why did he say it? Lonergan's theological method is intellectually rigorous, but he holds that *before* one can move from what has been said about God by others, to the forming of truths about God for oneself, there has to be a conversion. That is, a falling in love and a subsequent opening of the eyes and ears to that which lies beyond the boundaries of our present knowing.

Pannenberg is committed, on the other hand to the grounding of faith in reason alone and is opposed to any appeal to conversion for that implies a capitulation to feeling. I think Pannenberg is wrong. Conversion is necessary and essential to the process of religious knowing, without which people settle for a knowledge that lies only within the limits of their so-called objective experience.

Conversion brings forth a new perspective, be it a matter of many years or a few seconds, a single or multiple experience, and as such is essential to faith. Our belief, disbelief and re-belief are related to what we expect from experience. Or to put it another way, we all filter the data of experience and identity, what we see, in terms of acculturated presuppositions and assumptions. If a person does not believe in God, it is because any data that might be interpreted to indicate the presence of God is either ignored (filtered out) or labeled with malicious intent to point to something else. Inevitably, our reflection upon our experience has as a precondition certain primordial symbols, learned from birth, which dictate in a real way the possibilities of what we perceive in our experience. Those symbols are continued most significantly in our rituals.

Dean Holmes illustrates the effect of a conversion by describing an account by a black American, Harvard trained anthropologist Bennetta Jules-Rosette, concerning her conversion to an African native church, the church of John Maranke. In her fieldwork, Dr. Jules-Rosette visited Zaire and Zambia and there studied the church of John Maranke, a native sect grounded in Christian tradition and combined with African idiom. It is standard, in the study of any religion, for an anthropologist to participate, observe, and record the community's rituals in minute detail. The effect of this activity was to confront Dr. Jules-Rosette's primodial images with a different set of images. The new set was assimilated into her consciousness, causing a conflict in her perception of the meaning and value of life. Here was a people whose expectations of life were very different from her own. These expectations were grounded in a very powerful symbol system, which she perceived in their ritual. As she began to integrate these symbols into her own life, dissonance was created, and this resulted in an internal crisis or disorientation.

Amidst this dislocating experience, Dr. Jules-Rosette was led to accept the vision of the church of John Maranke and to begin the process of discarding her own primordial images and symbols so as to assimilate those of her new community. Dean Holmes says "begin," because she testifies again and again to the fact that the choice to convert is only the first step in learning a new reality. Conversion in one sense resolves the inner crisis, but only because it is a surrender to the possibility of a new awareness. It is the beginning of a long reorientation to a new reality. As a convert, she now lives *as if* the God of John Maranke exists, but she has yet to know *what* that is or means.

Her assimilation of new symbols led to a new order of thinking. The possibility of what may be known and what is known is now different than before her transformation.[1]

Milton Rokeach, the sociologist,[2] has discovered in his work on values that it is possible to bring about a dramatic and lasting change in values by bringing out the conflicts in the values people hold. It is possible to suppress the conflict by professing opposing values, but when the awareness of these conflicts is made painfully unavoidable, it is our nature to make a choice between them. It is then that persons become disciples.

Christian initiation, the incorporation of persons into Christian faith and life, necessitates this movement from orientation to disorientation to reorientation. The possibility of the integrated spiritual life of religious experience and prophetic action necessitates this reorientation or conversion. Ritual, I contend, is the primary context for this process. Catechesis, therefore, needs to focus its attention on the transformation of human lives.

Initiation

Death and resurrection, dying and becoming, describe best the experience of Christians.[3] If we do not believe in God, it is because any data that might be interpreted as the presence of God is either ignored or labeled to point to something else. The miracle of sight resides in our seeing anew that which we have overlooked. What we mean by revelation is an experience of breaking through the ordinary reality in which we live.

It is, therefore, important to remember that the purpose of catechesis is to open us to new insight. Catechesis is to be a transforming experience. Helen Keller's life thereby presents a paradigm for catechesis. On a summer day in 1887 she first apprehended the meaning of a word and as she wrote in her autobiography, "I saw everything with strange, new sight that had come to me."[4] Helen Keller's experience was that of a second birth. The word "water" had been lost and was found, and in the recovery of this word she was given new life.

We, too, hear without understanding and see without perceiving. The purpose of catechesis is to evoke the possibility of turning, of transformation, of new insight. Liturgy shares these concerns.

The genesis of a faith community is marked by the shared religious experience of its members—the resurrection of Jesus experienced by the disciples. But the passing of this founding generation means that the community of faith contains folk who have not had this original conversion. Indeed, in our culture, many are born within the community and never sense the power of a transformed existence. How are we moderns to become "live" members of a "living church"? More significant initiation rites could provide a context and stimulant for the transformation of consciousness and life. To understand their nature and character, let me describe a contemporary simple society on the continent of Africa and one from an ancient Christian community.[5]

The initiation ritual for young men in the simple society I am about to describe takes place every few years.

When the time is right the whole community engages in building a wall in the forest a short distance from the village. Once the wall is completed, passing beyond it is taboo. At the proper time, masked dancers round up the young men, pulling them toward the wall as their families strive to pull them toward the village. A bladder of chicken blood is tied to their chest. As they near the fence a spear is thrust into the bladder bathing each young man in blood. He falls to the ground as if dead and is tossed over the wall where he is caught just as a log is dropped to give the impression of his dead body hitting the ground. His family wails as the young man takes an oath of secrecy, participates in a sacrificial meal, is circumcized, and scarified with cuts on his chest and back to symbolize the teeth of the crocodile in whose stomach he is believed to live until his rebirth.

Then, over a period of two to three years he is taught all that he needs to know to function as an adult member of the tribe. During this period, as an act of hope, his parents build him a home, plant a garden for him, and make his clothing. When the young man's learning is complete, he is ready to be reincorporated into the community and returned to the village. But first comes an unmasking of the leaders and a ceremonial bath. The young man then returns to the village and wanders about as if a stranger until his parents find him and lead him to his new home, and a great feast is held to celebrate his rebirth.

Now that certainly makes contemporary initiation rites in mainline Protestant churches look somewhat bland, but initiation in the early church was just as dramatic.

In the first few centuries of the Christian era when an adult was converted to the Christian faith she was brought before the congregation by a sponsor who testified to her sincerity of desire to embrace the faith. The moral life of the candidate—catechumen—was then examined and if found worthy she was pronounced a Christian through the laying on of hands and the signing with the cross.

For the next two to three years the catechumen entered a preparation period intended to shape her life according to the Christian way. Besides participation in moral instruction she was expected to attend the weekly ritual of the community, but only for the first half. Following the reading of Scripture, the sermon and prayers, the catechumen exchanged the kiss of peace and was dismissed so as not to witness or participate in the celebration of the Lord's Supper. Periodically during these probationary years, the catechumen was brought before the congregation and examined. When she was considered ready, on the first Sunday of Lent she signed her name in the church register and the date of her baptism was set; namely the forthcoming Easter. During this period a more intense form of learning was conducted emphasizing the spiritual life and church dogma.

Participation in the Holy Week rituals marked the incorporation of the catechumen into the community of the faithful. Maundy Thursday was celebrated with exorcisims; Good Friday with prayers and fasting. Then, on Easter eve, the final ritual began. The catechumen was once again exorcised, her eyes, ears, and nose anointed with oil. She renounced the devil and made her profession of faith. The salvation story was told, and she stripped naked and was emerged in the coffin-like baptismal font to be baptized in the name of the Father, Son, and Holy Spirit. Coming out on the other side she was anointed with oil and put on a white garment. She then processed to the altar where the bishop confirmed her baptism and laid hands upon her. For the first time she participated in the Lord's Supper. Then, until Pentecost, she wore her baptismal garments, coming to church each day for the celebration of the Lord's Supper and to learn the meaning of the rites she had participated in. Thus ended the initiation ritual.

Today the church lacks such significant transforming rituals. In fact, it appears as if the church has abandonded rituals and left them in the hands of secular humanistic psychologists. A number of years ago I experienced one such significant rite at the Esalen Institute in Big Sur, California—a center of the human potential movement. It was through participation in this transforming rite that I and others were "converted" to understanding the unity of body and mind, the importance of the intuitional mode of consciousness, the character of true *communitas*, the integration of belief and action, and the nature of conversion.

In very broad outlines, let me describe that experience. The trip from New Jersey to Big Sur provided an initial separation from past status and regular patterns of interaction. The site was isolated and beautiful. I knew no one upon arrival, but this small group soon became a little world of its own. We introduced ourselves by first names only. We knew nothing about each other's past or present. (It was only at the end that we shared those aspects of our lives.) All of the rules defining who we were or how we were to relate to each other were suspended. Normally taboo behavior, such as touching, expressing emotion, or direct interpersonal confrontation was encouraged. Nude bathing in the hot sulfur baths amidst incense and candles, along with mineral oil massaging, began and ended each day.

Through highly structured, guided experience, we were confronted with our past understandings and ways and transformed into new ones. The week was a ritual event, a series of symbolic actions intended to convert us and equip us to be reformed as new persons. As a result, our world views and values were significantly changed. None of us have been the same since.

If we consider contemporary secularized American culture and Christian faith, a similar transformation is necessary for Christian life. To that extent we are very much like persons in the first centuries of the Christian era.

A challenge faces the church. Can we evolve a meaningful rite of Christian maturity? Baptism is *the* rite of Christian initiation. At our baptism we are made Christian and incorporated into Christ's church. Baptism needs to be given much greater importance and treated with greater seriousness. It would be well for us to celebrate our baptism day, and it is essential for each of us to renew our baptismal vows at every new baptism.

Confirmation, on the other hand, needs to be rethought. It has a confused and despicable history of being a ticket to communion, a Christian Bar (Bas) Mitzvah, a completion of baptism, and an announcement of church membership. Confirmation might better be understood as a rite of Christian maturity, a celebration of a commitment to witness in the world, and an empowerment by the Holy Spirit to struggle against the forces of evil.

We are Christians by our baptism and in various ways, but particularly at the renewal of our baptismal vows and our weekly participation in the Eucharist, we reaffirm our faith and commitment throughout our pilgrimage. Still we need to celebrate significant turning points in our lives, especially in our thirties and forties. Indeed, we need to make transitions and mark transformations if we are to experience Christian maturity in a secular world.

Confirmation could acknowledge a call to vocation, mark a personal decision for mission, signify an ordination to ministry, and celebrate a strengthening for Christian service in the world. As such, confirmation is a rite of commitment and responsibility which could reasonably be celebrated more than once in a person's adult life. Never a point of arrival or completion, confirmation celebrates a significant change in a person's faith pilgrimage and marks a new beginning.

If the church is to become a disciplined, intentional, faithful community, the transformation and commissioning of adults needs to be taken more seriously. Just imagine a two-year preparation for confirmation understood as ordination to ministry. Consider persons writing a covenant of concrete, specific intentions between themselves, the church, and God, which could be published weeks before confirmation—like wedding banns. Picture persons reading and signing their covenant in the presence of a congregation and then being sealed in that covenant and held accountable for its fulfillment.

Confirmation could become a sign of a significant transformation in peoples' lives and a public commitment to ministry. Then might not the church be on the way to becoming a renewed community of faith? Then might not the baptism of children and their nurturing in a Eucharistic community of celebration and mission begin to assume meaning and power?

We have a great deal to learn about ritual in the lives of persons and communities. We have a number of important theological issues to address. And we have a host of educational possibilities to imagine and explore. Liturgy and catechesis belong together. The future of the church's educational ministry and the church's mission are challenged by an awareness of their contemporary estrangement and historic union.

· 8 ·

Identity and the
Pilgrimage of Faith

For the Christian, baptism establishes Christian identity. Further, baptism is understood as a sacrament, that is, an initiation ritual in which God acts. Persons can oppose or resist God's action, but God's activity does not depend upon our doing. At baptism, the Christian believes that through the outward and visible sign of water, inward and spiritual grace is given by Christ, and persons are thereby adopted into a family. Baptism celebrates a new birth, a new life, and the giving of a new name—Christian. This insertion into "Christ's body," the church, creates a change intrinsic to the person's life. A person can reject or deny his or her adoption and its inheritance, but that does not change the fact of who and whose that person is.

Baptism is the means by which one becomes a Christian and a member of Christ's church. The Eucharist, the Lord's Supper or Holy Communion, is the sustaining rite of the Christian, the sacrament of continuing grace, a family thanksgiving meal of God and God's people. Baptism—and baptism alone—grants a person the right and privilege of participation in the Eucharist, an outward and visible sign in bread and wine of inward and spiritual grace. This Holy Communion sustains them and the community in Christian faith and life.

Confirmation is a sacramental act (necessary but not essential) whereby God grants, to those who recognize and affirm who and whose they are, God's spirit to assume and perform the ministry to which all those who have been baptized are called.

Surely it can be defended that these three—baptism, confirmation, and first communion—are properly celebrated together, either at birth or in adulthood. Properly, they can also be separated and celebrated over time. The history of these various practices is not a story of progress or evolution but of the various situations to which the church has responded in multiple faithful ways. To be faithful in our day, the church, once again will need to examine its practices and make a decision. Some Christians are convinced that our secular world calls for the radical act of returning to an adult catechumenate, with serious preparation for a combined baptism, confirmation, and first communion rite. (The Orthodox churches still affirm the significance of these combined rites at birth.) My preference is baptism with communion at birth; first communion, after preparation, at the time when a baptized child requests it; the establishment of a new adolescent rite of responsibility; and adult confirmation or the ordination of the laity for ministry, some of whom will be called and ordained to priesthood, best understood as a sacramental ministry focused on the administration of community rites and rituals. The following suggested educational program is based upon this formulation.

Remember, one thing we can learn from the history of the church's original adult initiation rite combining baptism, confirmation, and first communion, and the subsequent history of these important rites, is that various choices have been made to address changing situations. For too long we have tried to argue from precedent: the early church did or did not baptize children, therefore, we should or should not do so; the early church had a single initiation rite, therefore, we should or should not do likewise. Baptism, confirmation, and first communion have been placed in various orders to meet new situations. Each generation, in its social context has had to make a decision on how it will celebrate its faith and initiate persons into its life. I would like to argue for baptism at birth, first communion in early childhood, a new rite in early adolescence, and confirmation in adulthood as a faithful sequence for Christians living in the United States in the last quarter of the twentieth century. My reasons for this decision are based upon my understanding of how rituals function in human growth, my understanding of faith development, and the theological-cultural situation in which the church finds itself today.

Faith, as I am using the word, represents the centered behaviors of persons, embodying their minds (beliefs), hearts (affections), and wills (actions) expressed through their lives in accordance with their growth or development. Faith, as such, is a verb. The activity of "faithing" has no age bounds but appears to express itself in characteristic, identifiable ways (styles) at differing points in a person's faith pilgrimage. (See chart p. 000)

1. Faith is a verb, a way of behaving which involves knowing, being, and willing; it is deeply personal and dynamic, a centered act of personality encompassing our hearts, minds, and wills according to our growth and development.
2. While each person's faith has its own unique characteristics, generalizations concerning the pilgrimage of faith can be described in terms of style.
   a. We do not give a child faith. A child has faith at birth. While the content of our faith is acquired through our interactions with other faithing

Affiliative Faith
(Childhood)

Belonging parti-
cipation/engagement
in service for others a
sense of community

Experienced Faith
(Early Childhood)

Observe/copy
(Acquiring role models
and foundations for
the integrity of belief
and action

Act/react
(Formation of trust)

Explore/test (Roots of
openness or closeness)

Affections/religion of
the heart dominates - a
strong desire and need
for significant religious
experiences

Authority/our story
and way—a search for
conviction; the
establishment of a firm
set of beliefs, attitudes,
and values. Learning
who and whose we
are.

Searching Faith
(Adolescence)

Commitment to
idealogy/engagement
in related action

Intellect/religion of
the head dominates -
the search for
understanding and
truth

Critical judgment of
the tradition nurtured
in; questioning and
growing doubt/
experimentation with
alternatives, experi-
ences the dark night of
the soul.

Mature Faith
(Adulthood)

Personal belief/a clear
sense of personal
identity with openness
to others.

Witness/religion of the
will dominates.

Centeredness/integrity
of belief and action

Note: Each style of faith has its own character, but builds on characteristics of earlier styles so that as growth occurs faith
becomes more complex. The process is slow, gradual, and
related to the presence of environments which nurture development and growth.

Experience Faith (Early Childhood)	Affiliative Faith (Childhood)	Searching Faith (Adolescence)
	A significant religious experience, since the 19th century in America called conversion. Tends to be a sudden, dramatic, intense, emotional experience resulting from a call to new life and incorporation into a community conscious of what it believes and how it should live; typical of older children and adolescence though not restricted to these ages; an affirmation of affiliative faith and a dramatic meeting of its characteristic needs.	Conversions as historically understood emerge in the midst of questioning and doubt (what some experience as the dark night of the soul). These conversions are experienced as illuminations resulting in new ways of "seeing and hearing." Sometimes initially dramatic, they typically involve a gradual process; sometimes emotional, but also always intellectual; rarely a single experience, typically multiple; the result of the witness of faithful folk, they typically occur during late adolescence and throughout adulthood as persons make a transition from searching to mature faith and grow in mature faith.

Mature Faith
(Adulthood)

Note: Some persons who have grown into mature faith have had the conversion experiences related to affiliative faith and some have not. All persons with mature faith have experienced one or more of the conversions characterized by the growth from searching to mature faith.

selves, a person's faith can expand, that is, become more complex. Expanded faith is not greater faith and, therefore, one's style of faith is not to be judged.

b. The style of our faith is not directly related to our age. That is, faith expands only if a proper environment exists. If this environment does not exist, faith ceases to expand until the proper environment is established.

c. Faith's expansion is slow and gradual, moving systematically over time to acquire additional characteristics. It cannot be speeded up beyond its normal rate of growth, nor can characteristics of its various styles be avoided or passed over.

d. The expansion of faith into new styles does not eliminate the faith needs of previous styles of faith. Rather, as it expands it only becomes more complex. If, therefore, the needs of early styles of faith are denied or neglected, a person will strive to meet those needs until all are satisfied.

e. From a Christian perspective, God's grace is freely given to all. Though it is our potential to expand in faith, we do not earn anything by so doing. Indeed, the desire to expand in faith is, for Christians, only an act of gratitude for the gift given.

f. We cannot manipulate or determine another's faith. At best we can encourage and support it and its expansion. At worst we can make that expansion more difficult. What is important is our own witness to faith and to the interaction of faithing persons in community.

Affiliative faith is typical of childhood, though it is not restricted to those years. Indeed, vast numbers of adults express their faith essentially through this style, either because its needs have not been satisfactorily met or because they have not been provided the necessary encouragement and environment to move beyond it. Still, even as our faith expands, we never seem to outgrow the characteristic needs of this or any other style of faith. That is, the needs of every evolving developmental style remains with us for life, and if we cease to meet these needs, no matter how far our faith has expanded, we will return to this style of faith until its needs are once again met.

Affiliative faith has three distinctive characteristics. First and foremost, it is faith centered in the affections. It is expressed as a religion of the heart more than of the head or will. Persons with affiliative faith further seek their identity in the authority of a community's understandings and ways; similarly, they long for belonging participation and service in the community's life. Persons are dependent upon the community for the content and shape of their faith, and they need to experience and image through nurture and ritual the community's understandings and ways. Through memories told and lived, roots are established; through creative expression the affections are nurtured, and visions of a purposeful future emerge; through trusting, caring, affirming, accepting interactions, self-worth and identity are framed and the present is made meaningful. These needs cannot be neglected or denied. The best way to understand youth's interest today in the variety of cults is that they provide a sense of community, intense religious experience, and, in a world of pluralism, a set of beliefs which claim ultimate truth.

There is no specific time span, identical for all persons, to satisfy these foundational needs of faith; nor do we ever outgrow their requirements. I suppose that more than half of all those going through the social condition of adolescence live within the limited perimeters of this faith style, as do many adults. Therefore, our ritual life needs to be expressive of this style of faith and speak to its needs, not only for the sake of those persons whose faith is affiliative, but for us all, including those who have moved beyond its bounds.

Providing that the needs of affiliative faith have been met satisfactorily, some time during the adolescent years a person can begin to acquire a new style of faith, that is, can begin to expand her or his faith to include new characteristics. This new faith style I have characterized as "searching faith."

Searching faith is marked as a time when the religion of the head begins to predominate over the religion of the heart. The mind begins to search for intellectual justifications of faith. Critical judgment of the community's understandings and ways, as well as short-term multiple commitments to ideologies and actions, emerge as persons strive to discover convictions worth living and dying for; that is, they learn what it means to give their lives away and live according to their convictions.

Having been "given" an identity during the childhood years, adolescents, in searching faith, struggle to find their own identity, and in so doing they typically experience the "darknight of the soul." Often unverbalized questions—such as: What is truth? Who am I? What communities are worth belonging to? What causes are worth living for?—dominate life's joyous troubling, liberating-confusing days and nights. Still, persons in searching faith long to belong, especially to a community which shares their concerns for passionate action, critical thought, and experimentation. While they struggle with and condemn the structural authority of the community, they long for moral, sapiential, charismatic, or personal authority. These are the betwixt-and-between years, when the social conditions of adolescence, which throw the individual into a state of limbo between childhood and adulthood (a period that can extend from thirteen to thirty), unite with the ordeal and liminality of searching faith. These are the years when it may appear that faith is lost and the community's nurturing has failed. And these are the years when a person appears to have matured into adulthood one day and the next to have regressed to early childhood. Difficult for both the individual and the community, these years of anxiety and storm must come before faith can assume its fullest dimensions.

This God-given potential for faith I have characterized as "mature faith." This is the faith of adulthood, but not necessarily of all adults, for it appears that only those who have moved through searching faith can acquire its characteristics of centeredness and personal identity. Persons with mature faith are secure enough in their convictions to stand against their community of nurture when conscience dictates. Having begun as a heteronomous self and moved to autonomy, the theonomous self emerges. Still in need of community, persons with mature faith reveal themselves to be inner-directed, open to others, but clear and secure in their own faith identity. Concerned to eliminate the dissonances between rhetoric and life, the religion of the will, with its witness to faith in deed and word predominates over the religion of heart or mind, although it encompasses both. Integrity of belief and action are realized.

Of course mature faith is always expanding; it is not to be understood as a state of arrival or conclusion. New depth and breadth emerge. Importantly, the needs and characteristics of earlier styles of faith continue. Doubt and the intellectual quest never end. Nor does the need to belong, to have the affections nurtured, or a sense of authority disappear, though they do express themselves somewhat differently. Indeed, if these various faith needs are not met, a person who has reached mature faith will return to an earlier style of faith until its needs are once again satisfied. Thus faith is never static.

For example, to grow into searching faith, persons need to have been given a sense of self-esteem and worth. They need to have learned to accept their strengths and weaknesses, to live in the hope that they will continue to grow, and to possess self-confidence. They need to have learned that they are adequate to meet the future. During the childhood years persons will, it is hoped, have experienced the grace of God in a sacramental community where the authority of the Word and the conviction that Jesus is Lord is lived in the intimacy of a belonging, caring fellowship. To have a sense of oneness with God, to feel loved for nothing, to know that you are understood and valued, are the gifts of a Christian community expressed through their common life and rituals.

However, for many adolescents, even those brought up in the church, the experience of loneliness, self-hatred, family conflict, estrangement, insecurity, close-mindedness, dogmatic authority, and an affection-less environment have made searching faith difficult to attain. In spite of their adolescent social condition, they need a community which nurtures affiliative faith.

Those, however, who have begun to move into searching faith need a community of social concern and action; a community whose rituals unite head and heart with a concern for justice; a community in which critical intellectual judgment is encouraged, doubt affirmed, and experimentation permitted. In some cases persons have been forced out of the church in order to meet these needs. This is especially unfortunate, for these persons still need belonging participation in a passionate community secure in its story and ways.

Life is not static. We each need to be prepared for new conditions, and the communities of which we are apart need to have ways to reestablish equilibrium following each change in the life of one of its members. Further, a new generation needs to be prepared for and given an understanding of the changes that are part of individual and community life. A community's rites and rituals serve these important functions.

Transition Rites

There is a category of rites which is known by some as the rites of passage, transition, or life crisis. Instead of following the calendar as rites of community do, these rites address the changes of our lives. Some correspond to biological changes such as birth, puberty, and death; and others to social changes such as marriage, graduation, and retirement. Such moments of changed role or status are traumatic to both individuals and the community. Ritual aids us to make these changes purposeful; they reestablish order in the community and help others to understand the possibility and meaning of change.[1]

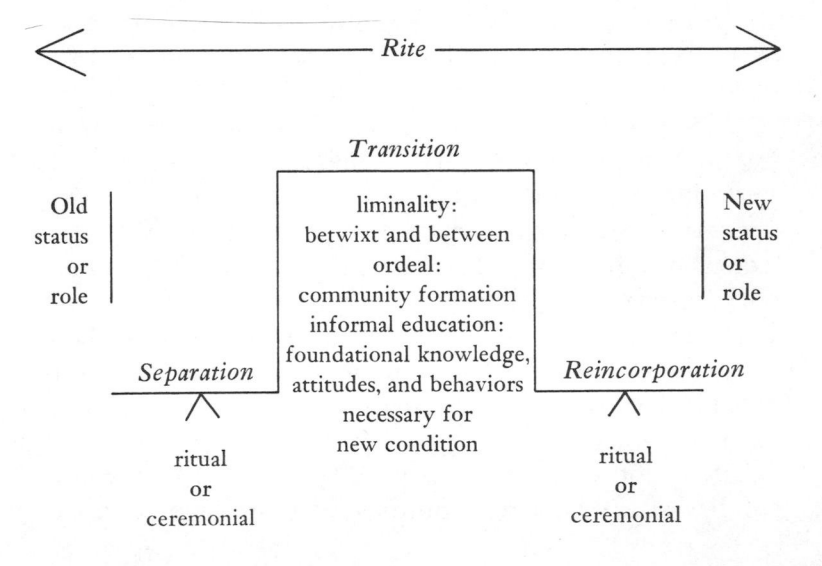

Rites of transition are comprised of three stages: separation, transition, and reincorporation. The rite properly begins and ends with a ceremonial or ritual. The second ritual telescopes these three stages into a single ceremony. For example, the rite of marriage begins with a ceremonial, the engagement, and ends after the honeymoon. The ritual of marriage (incorporating these three stages) is the wedding ceremony, which begins with the couple separated, continues with their coming together to announce their intentions, making a series of promises and being pronounced husband and wife. The ritual ends as they are blessed and depart together to be integrated into the community as a married couple.

To return to the styles in a life-crisis rite, once the separation from one's status or role is realized, and before one is reincorporated into the community with a new status or role, an important period of transition occurs. It is, first of all, a period of liminality—limbo— in which a person experiences a state of being betwixt and between; in this case neither married nor single. Once a person's engagement is announced, old friends proceed with caution, checking out the appropriateness of old behaviors. During this period the engaged couple experiences being set apart, that is, they are not typically invited either to the parties of married couples or to those of their old single friends. Normal interaction has been reduced and all the appropriate behaviors of the past have been suspended, while future appropriate behaviors are inappropriate. If this period of transition is too short, or lacks the dynamic of an ordeal, the marriage and the role-status of wife and husband are apt to be less secure. The gift of this ordeal is an experience of community, but the most important aspect of this transition period is "education." It is the time to acquire the understandings and ways of behavior (thinking, feeling, acting) appropriate to the person's new state or role.

Typically, this education is informal: for example, an engagement party. In the past a woman's mother would hold a party for her daughter and other women. They would bring gifts such as kitchen utensils and exchange recipes. Today women sometimes get mixed signals and confused learning. That is, their friends also may hold a coed party and give an apron and recipes to the fiancee.

To give one further example, of a life-crisis rite; at one time, "the last rites" functioned as a ceremony of separation. During the ordeal and liminal period between that ceremony and the funeral, the person's kin and friends were prepared for death. The funeral then ritualized the person's rebirth into that new state the church believes exists for persons among the community of saints. I first became aware of these dynamics when I served a parish in New England. We could not bury people in the winter months. A tragic, unexpected death in the winter, with its winter funeral and spring burial ceremony, seemed to result in better family adjustments than for those who suffered the same sort of tragic death in the spring months, when both funeral and burial were celebrated at the same time. It was then that I realized how important this liminal state could be if informal education or preparation was provided.

Education is always a central aspect of transition rites. Persons need to be prepared for their new status and role. Such informal learning properly includes only that basic knowledge (understanding), attitudes (sensibilities), and skills (behaviors) required by their new condition. This does not mean they need to rehearse all past learnings or to learn everything they will ever need to know. Only foundational learning for life in their new state is necessary or proper.

Typically informal learning during initiation takes place away from the initiate's home. It lasts as long as necessary to insure that the initiate is fully prepared for her or his new role or status. Most importantly, the educational methods used for learning are "symbolic" in nature. For example: through dance boys and girls perform symbolic sexual acts; girls and boys rehearse adult roles through games; youth are tested on their knowledge of the community's understandings through puzzles and riddles; through corporate living in simulated settings, songs, dances, and sacred stories youth learn the meaning of community life.

What follows is a series of models. They are meant to be more suggestive than prescriptive. Each educational component will be best achieved through informal, natural interactions of persons, in contrast to formal schooling-instructional programs. Each will also have its unique characteristic consistent with the cultural ways and needs of the people involved. There is a mystery to the pilgrimage of faith and life in the Christian faith community. It cannot be programmed or organized as to age or any other particular. And especially important is the acknowledgment that they are dependent upon the faith and life of the church's confirmed members.

Rites of Christian Identity

Christians are made, not born.[2] Identity and transition during faith's pilgrimage are a central issue for the church. Just as membership in the old Israel was never a matter of nature or birth (Israel was adopted by God to be God's people), membership in the new Israel was by an act of God. Baptism celebrated that fact in the early church. That is, baptism was understood as a symbolic, sacramental act whereby God adds persons to God's eschatological community. That is, baptism—the same initiation rite for men and women, unique in the history of religions—is the means by which a person is adopted into an existing community.

Parenthetically, let me say that in most societies there is a different initiation rite for men and women and that the male rite is considered the most significant. Within the Christian community it is radically different. Both men and women share the same initiation rite—baptism. Thus it is that Christian faith makes the revolutionary statement that men and women are equal and in the eyes of God there is no male or female, Jew or Greek, adult or child, for in the church they are all one in Christ. Regretfully, this is an essential affirmation of the Christian faith that has yet to be actualized in our corporate life.

Baptism is in and of itself the central rite of Christian initiation. It is a sacrament in which God is the chief actor. In baptism the Christian church celebrates its conviction that God loves us for nothing (grace). Before we can make any response to God, God acts for our good through physical objects and actions. Later we can oppose or resist, but God's action does not depend on either our acceptance or worthiness. By God's action we are incorporated into that tradition-bearing community which proclaims its faith through word and deed. Still, for this radical action of God to be realized we need to make some response. That is why the norm for the church's initiation rite is adult baptism. However, the church historically has been concerned about the children of the faithful, nurtured within a faith community. This concern resulted in child baptism.

The church is best understood as a family of the baptized and their kin. Through baptism a person is adopted and incorporated into the community of faith. This explains why exceptions are rightly made for the children of the faithful when they (parents or sponsors) are committcd and able to raise their children within the household of faith.

Baptism, in any case, is adoption into a new family, a new birth, and the acquisition of a new name. It is as radical an act as that of a child being born to American upper-class parents in New York City and then immediately transported to be raised by poor Brazilian peasants.

The Lord's Supper, the Eucharist or Holy Communion, is the sustaining rite of the Christian community. It makes real the continuing gift of God's grace celebrated at baptism. Baptism makes a person a full member of the church and is the only necessary condition for acceptance at the Lord's table. However, it appears wise to wait until a person desires to commune and participate in this family meal. Therefore, first communion is a decision of the child, granted, after preparation by the child's parents.

Confirmation may be inappropriate for early adolescence. A more meaningful rite can to be created. I am suggesting a covenant of discipleship rite. Youth need to assume responsibility for their own faith; they need to struggle with the faith of their parents and community; they need to explore alternatives and critically judge their heritage. A new rite appears necessary if the pilgrimage of faith and life in the Christian faith community is to be meaningful.

Only if the adolescent pilgrimage has been affirmed and encouraged can persons in early adulthood be prepared for confirmation, perhaps best understood as a rite of Christian maturity characterized by a "conversion" or transformation, which is understood as enlightenment or illumination. At confirmation persons celebrate their coming to mature faith and commit themselves to Christian ministry. While the pilgrimage of faith continues, a new start has begun.

For those who did not begin their pilgrimage at birth, baptism, first communion, and confirmation can be united into a single rite of initiation following serious and lengthy (two or more years) preparation.

Baptism

When persons know that they are to have a child by birth or adoption, they and their mates, where there is a mate, might come before the congregation to announce and celebrate this event. As part of this celebration, sponsors may be called forth from among the faithful of the congregation and commissioned to prepare the parent(s) for the presence of a child.

In the informal setting of weekly evening meals (for nine months), amidst prayers and the reading of Scripture, the sponsors and parent(s) might do the following: (1) seriously examine the baptismal liturgy, exploring its meaning and the promises to be made; (2) share in an honest discussion of the faith and spiritual life of the parent(s), their beliefs and doubts, their devotional and liturgical life; and (3) engage in experiences and learnings related to the healthy mental and spiritual care of a child (learning to massage a child or adult with perfumed oil, for instance). Every few months the parents and sponsors might come before the congregation to share their pilgrimage and ask for the community's prayers and support.

If this is a second child, these learnings can be addressed to the other children as well as the parents so that a whole family is prepared for the presence of a new member; obviously, this is also an opportunity to help children understand their own baptism.

Should the child die before birth, a supportive community has been created. Should the child live, the parents are prepared for their child's baptism which also is, properly, a renewal of their own and the congregation's baptismal vows. Correspondingly, the church could celebrate baptism days as well as birthdays to emphasize the centrality and importance of this sacrament in the life of the church.

First Communion

Rightly, baptism should be a community celebration in the context of the Eucharist. It would, therefore, seem appropriate to share the wine and bread of the Eucharist with the newly baptized child, an act later to be recalled and celebrated.

It is to be expected that children will share in the church's weekly liturgy with their parents. However, while they receive the sacrament of Holy Communion at their birth, they might not commune again until they express a desire to do so, and then only after a period of preparation.

On that special occasion when they express a desire to commune (regardless of age), the priest should announce this happy moment, give them special recognition, and have the congregation express its joy. The children should then be reminded of their participation in the Eucharist at their baptism and be encouraged to prepare for their first desired communion. Parents should be commissioned to prepare their children for their first communion.

During the next weeks in the informal context of regular family life they should be prepared. This preparation might include the following: (1) Through the sharing of bedtime stories they might learn that the church is a family, that a sign points to something else (for example, a red light means stop), that love is being affirmed and accepted as they are, that Jesus Christ is the sign of God's love, that eating gives us more than food (it nourishes us), and that the Eucharist is a family thanksgiving meal with Jesus at which we celebrate God's love. (2) They might learn how the community shares in this family meal by observing and questioning their parents during the weekly celebration and by being recognized as being in preparation for their first communion. And (3) they could further be encouraged to help set the table at home, light the dinner candles, bake bread and make wine and, just before their first communion, help to prepare the holy table for the sacrament. On their first communion day, they could help to prepare the bread and wine and help their parents to bring this offering to the altar.

On the first communion day, children could be presented to the congregation, given the gift of a Bible and prayer book and be applauded for their decision to participate in the weekly meal of their family in Christ, the family they were adopted into at baptism. In this regard it might be appropriate to celebrate their first communion on their baptism day if at all reasonable.

A Covenant of Discipleship

Thirteen, the beginning of the teen years, is an important turning point in the life of every person. It is a time when they are ready to, and indeed need to, begin to assume responsibility for their life and faith. During the preceding years, their parents and community have nurtured them in Christian faith. Now they are ready to enter a new period of responsibility in their faith pilgrimage.

This is a time when adults, and older youth who have recently made their covenant, might join together in the preparation of these new teen-agers. On their twelfth

baptism day, they might celebrate their decision to prepare for this new stage in their life. On their thirteenth
baptism day they might make their covenant of discipleship. During this ensuing year their preparation, joined
in by others where appropriate, should be individually
tailored to their needs but aim for the following: (1) to
acquire critical skills of biblical study including possibly
Greek or Hebrew; (2) to learn about religious alternatives such as Hare Krishna or Unification Church; (3) to
be helped to understand the church as it is, be given a
vision of what it is called to become, and be enabled to
acquire skills for reforming the church; (4) in the context
of a series of retreats, to be helped to gain a sense of what
it means to be a learner, to make a covenant (a promise
to assume adult responsibility for their faith), and to
explore their faith and doubts through the lives of the
saints; and (5) to learn what it means to assume responsibility for ministry in the church by assisting in parish
calls, serving the needy, helping with the altar guild,
ushering, reading the lessons, and praying the prayers in
the morning liturgy.

On their baptism day a year after they began their
preparation they might be presented by their parents to
the congregation. The young man or woman might read
the lessons and give the homily. They could then make
a covenant to assume responsibility for their own faith
and promise to struggle with the faith of the community
until they understood it and could confirm it for themselves. They might be presented with a St. Thomas (the
doubter) cross, and their parents might pray, "Thank
you God for relieving us of the burden of responsibility
for our child's faith." Following the Eucharist, the congregation could hold a special dinner, celebration, and
party for the young man or woman, at which they might
assume adult responsibility for the blessing.

Confirmation

Confirmation is best understood, I believe, as an adult rite, the ordination of the laity to ministry. Ideally it would occur during early adulthood, but could be celebrated any time a person is ready. More than likely this would occur when a person was between thirty and forty. When they decide to prepare for their confirmation, this event could be celebrated during the Sunday liturgy, and sponsors could be called forth from among the faithful to prepare them. The time of preparation would vary from person to person, but would include knowledge, awareness, and skills related to all the functions of ministry: For example: social action, as prophetic political action in the society, contributes to God's community-building; evangelism, as the church living and proclaiming its faith in God's good news; stewardship, as the church expressing God's will for individual and corporate life in the world; worship, as the church celebrating its faith and being empowered for mission; pastoral care, as the church ministering to the material and spiritual needs of all people; community life, as the church providing a sign of God's coming community; organization and administration, as the church directing its life so that it can best fulfill its mission and ministry.

This education would ideally take place in the context of performing these ministries with those who are engaged in them within the church and reflecting upon each in the light of the church's faith. Serious study of Scripture, church history, theology, and ethics would be integrated into learning for ministry.

The final preparation might occur during Lent when, during a series of retreats, their spiritual life, faith, and vocation could be explored. Then on Maundy Thursday they might be dismissed before the Lord's Supper to begin a retreat with their sponsor. From then till Easter they would fast. On Good Friday, following the adoration of the Cross, they would help to cover (or bury) the crosses, put out the candles (celebrate the church's death) and build a camp fire outside the church where on Holy Saturday they might gather to retell the story of our faith. Then on Easter eve they would be reminded of their baptism and participate in the Easter liturgy, lead the congregation into the church with their lighted candles, uncover the crosses and prepare the table for celebration of the rebirth of the church and, in a special ceremony, be confirmed, that is, celebrate their decision to assume a ministry in the Christian church, and then be the first to receive the Holy Communion as their empowering food for mission.

These are just a few images of possible efforts at integrating liturgy and catechesis. Numerous problems remain, but perhaps new insight and stimulus have been provided for the church's educational ministry.

Notes

PREFACE

1. While each of John Westerhoff's essays were written for this book, the contents of some were presented earlier in other forms. These sources are acknowledged gratefully: "Learning and Prayer," *Religious Education*, September-October 1975; "The Liturgical Imperative in Religious Education," J. M. Lee (ed.), *The Religious Education We Need* (Mishawaka, Indiana: Religious Education Press, 1977); "Betwixt and Between," *Liturgy*, September 1977; "Spirituality: Revelation, Myth and Ritual," Gloria Durka and Joanmarie Smith (eds.), *The Other Side of Religious Education* (New York: Paulist Press, 1978); and "Joining the Church or Witnessing to Faith," *Character Potential*, 1978.

INTRODUCTION

1. See Gwen Kennedy Neville, "Religious Socialization of Women in U.S. Sub-Cultures" in Alice Hageman (ed.), *Sexist Religion and Women in the Church* (New York: Association Press, 1974). Also see articles on learning and culture in John H. Westerhoff, III, and Gwen Kennedy Neville, *Generation to Generation* (Philadelphia: Pilgrim Press, 1974).

CHAPTER ONE

1. The data for this analysis were collected in three field trips to Scotland (1972, 1975, and 1977) and in a number of research projects in the American South (1970–77). Ethnographic methods were augmented by the use of local archives and materials in the University of Edinburgh Library of the School of Scottish Studies, University of Edinburgh, and the libraries of Emory and Duke Universities.

2. Quoted by Charles Read Baskerville, "Dramatic Aspects of Medieval Folk Festivals in England"; reprinted from *Studies in Philology* 17, 1, (January 1920):23.

3. Nora Chadwick, *Celtic Britain* (London: Thames & Hudson, 1963).

4. J. G. Brown, *Religious Life in Southwest Scotland Since 1560* (Castle Douglas, Scotland: Broughton House Exhibition, 1960).

5. John F. Robertson, *The Story of Galloway* (Castle Douglas, Scotland: J. H. Maxwell, Ltd., 1963), p. 153.

6. Ibid., p. 170.

7. James Barr, *The Scottish Covenanters* (Glasgow, Scotland: John Smith & Son. 1947), p. 175.

8. Douglas C. Edmiston, "Communion Tokens," *Scottish Field*, April 1974, p. 1 (reproduced for a museum exhibit in Kirkudbright, Scotland: The Stewartry Museum).

9. J. J. Vernon, *The Parish and Kirk of Hawick 1711–1725*, The Hawick Express Reprint Series (Hawick, Scotland: The Hawick Express, 1900).

10. James Russell, *Reminiscences of Yarrow* (Edinburgh, Scotland: William Blackwood & Sons, 1886), p. 172.

11. Ibid., p. 177

12. Ibid., p. 8
13. Attributed to a man named "Principal Shairp of Hawick," quoted in Vernon, p. 45.
14. J. McElroy, *Seven Kirks in the Stewartry* (Castle Douglas, Scotland: Printed by J. McElroy, 1971).
15. James Tait, *Two Centuries of Border Church Life* (Kelso, Scotland: Printed by J. McElroy, 1971).
16. Ibid., p. 34.
17. Many fine histories exist which document this wave of settlement and its religious dimensions. See, for example, James G. Leyburn, *The Scotch-Irish: A Social History* (Chapel Hill: University of North Carolina Press, 1962); E. T. Thompson, *Presbyterians in the South* (Richmond: John Knox Press, 1963); William Warren Sweet, *The Story of Religion in America* (New York, 1930).
18. For a detailed treatment of the campmeeting tradition see Walter Brownlow Posey, *Frontier Mission: A History of Religion West of the Southern Appalachians to 1861* (Lexington: University of Kentucky Press, 1966) and Dickenson Bruce, *And They All Sang Hallelujah—Plain-Folk Camp-Meeting Religion 1800–1840* (Knoxville: University of Tennessee Press, 1975).

CHAPTER TWO

1. Coauthor of this chapter is Jack G. Hunnicutt, Jr., who has kindly consented for it to be included here. Another version of this same material will appear as a chapter in a collection of readings edited by Solon Kimball and tentatively titled *Plain Folk in the Mainstream South*.
2. See Marion Pearsall, "Cultures of the American

South," *Anthropological Quarterly* 39 (April 1966): 128–141; also Frank Lawrence Owsley, *Plain Folk of the Old South* (Baton Rouge: Louisiana State University Press, 1949).

3. For other work utilizing this same approach, see Gwen Kennedy Neville, *Annual Assemblages and the Persistence of Culture Patterns: An Anthropological Study of a Summer Community* (Ann Arbor, Michigan: University Microfilms, 1971); Gwen Kennedy Neville and Jack G. Hunnicutt, Jr., "Community Form and Ceremonial Life in Three Regions of Scotland," *American Ethnologist* (accepted for publication 1978). Grounding for these ideas is found in the work of Warner, Arensberg, and Kimball: W. Lloyd Warner, *The Family of God: A Symbolic Study of Christian Life in America* (New Haven: Yale University Press, 1965); Conrad M. Arensberg and Solon T. Kimball, *Culture and Community* (New York: Harcourt, Brace & World, Inc., 1965).

4. The data for this analysis were collected in three phases: (1) open-ended interviews were conducted in order to elicit the informant categories for the family and church assemblies we wished to identify; (2) On the basis of the first phase, a survey questionnaire form was constructed and administered to 202 respondents, divided approximately equally among the three denominations of Methodist, Baptist, and Presbyterian; (3) The authors attended as participant observers as many of the gatherings as could be found and to which access could be arranged. We would like to express our appreciation to all of our informants and students who have participated in this project over the years.

5. An interesting approach to family ritual is taken by von Mering, who calls the everyday, regularized in-

teractions in a family "behavioral pieties." See Otto von Mering, "Iterative Activity and Behavioral Piety in Private Places," *Learning and Culture:* 1973 Proceedings of the American Ethnological Society, Solon T. Kimball and Jacquetta Burnett (eds.).

6. Ayoub has studied family reunions in the Midwest and has classified her findings into three types: cognate reunion, sibling reunion, and name reunion. We find some similarities to the types she labels "cognate reunion" and "sibling reunion." The southern family, however, resembles a classical descent group more closely than does the family described for the Midwest. (See Milicent Ayoub, "The Family Reunion," *Ethnology* 5:415–33.)

7. Quoted in Dorothy Russell, "A Southern Family," unpublished paper presented to the seminar on the anthropology of the American South at Emory University, May 1977.

8. See footnote 18, chapter one.

CHAPTER THREE

1. This chapter was originally published as an article in *Liturgy,* October 1974, entitled "Baptism in Cultural Context."

2. Arnold van Gennep, *Les Rites de passage* (Paris: Emile Nourry, 1909).

3. See Victor Turner, *The Ritual Process* (Chicago: Aldine Publishing Company, 1969).

CHAPTER FOUR

1. Edward B. Tylor, known to many as "the father of anthropology," first defined culture in 1871 as follows: ". . . that complete whole, including beliefs,

habits, customs, values, that man learns as a part of a society" (*Primitive Culture,* 2 vols. [London: J. Murray, 1903]).

2. See also Gwen Kennedy Neville, "Marginal Communicant: The Anthropoligist in Religious Groups and Agencies" in Elizabeth Eddy et al. (eds.), *Applied Anthropology in America* (New York: Columbia University Press, 1978); and Morris Frielich *Marginal Natives: Anthropologists at Work* (Harper & Row: New York, 1970).

CHAPTER FIVE

1. I gratefully acknowledge this particular expression of the Christian story to my friend Gabriel Fackre, professor of theology at Andover Newton Theological Seminary.

2. Numerous resources for this sort of catechesis exist. For example, see Loren B. Mead, ed., *Celebrations of Life* (New York: Seabury Press, 1974); and Gabe Huck and Virginia Sloyan, *Parishes and Families* (Washington, D.C.: The Liturgical Conference, 1973). Also see *Major Feasts and Seasons* from the Liturgical Conference and the seasonal guides from the Glenmary Home Missioners.

CHAPTER SIX

1. Idries Shah, *The Exploits of the Incomparable Mulla Nasrudin* (New York: E.P. Dutton, 1972), p. 18.

2. One of the most important books written in this decade is Urban T. Holmes, *Ministry and Imagination* (New York: Seabury Press, 1977). Better than any work I know, it helps us to understand this dimension of reality.

3. Albert Cullum, *The Geranium on the Windowsill Just Died but Teacher You Went Right On* (New York: Harlin Quist, 1971), p. 14.
4. Gordon D. Kaufman, *God The Problem* (Cambridge, Ma.: Harvard University Press, 1972).
5. Ibid., p. 219.
6. See H. Richard Niebuhr, *The Meaning of Revelation* (New York: Macmillan, 1946).
7. Jan Chiapusso, *Bach's World* (Bloomington, In.: Indiana University Press, 1968), p. 141.
8. Amos Niven Wilder, *Theopoetic* (Philadelphia: Fortress Press, 1976). This book makes a significant contribution to catechesis and ought not to be ignored.
9. Thomas Merton, *Contemplation in a World of Action* (Garden City, N.Y.: Image Books, 1973), p. 173.

CHAPTER SEVEN

1. This illustration and comment come from Dean Urban T. Holmes. I am indebted to him for this insight which appears in detail in our new book in the Episcopal Church's Teaching Series, *Christian Believing*.
2. See Milton Rokeach, *The Nature of Human Values* (New York: Free Press, 1973).
3. I am indebted to my friend Malcolm L. Warford, author of *The Necessary Illusion* (Philadelphia: Pilgrim Press, 1976), for his insight on "Metanoia: A Way of Thinking about Christian Education," which first appeared in *New Conversations* (vol. 2, no. 2, Fall 1977), and from which I adopted these thoughts.
4. Helen Keller, *The Story of My Life* (Garden City, N.Y.: Doubleday, 1954), p. 24.

5. The initiation rite from the **Poro** people of Liberia was recounted to me by a student at Duke from Liberia. For initiation rites in the early church, see Dom Gregory Dix, *The Shape of the Liturgy* (London: Dacre Press, 1945).

CHAPTER EIGHT

1. Transition rites as studies by anthropologists provide us with important insights. See Victor Turner, *The Ritual Process* (New York: Aldine, 1969); and Arnold van Gennep, *The Rites of Passage* (Chicago: University of Chicago Press, 1960).

2. See Mircea Eliade, *Rites and Symbols of Initiation* (New York: Harper & Row, 1958); Murphy Center for Liturgical Research, *Made, Not Born* (Notre Dame, In.: University of Notre Dame Press, 1976); Urban T. Holmes, *Young Children and the Eucharist* (New York: Seabury Press, 1976); Urban T. Holmes, *Confirmation* (New York: Seabury Press, 1975); John Hines, *By Water and the Holy Spirit* (New York: Seabury Press, 1973).